Reinventing London

Series editor: Diane Coyle

Reinventing London

Bridget Rosewell

LONDON PUBLISHING PARTNERSHIP

Published by London Publishing Partnership
www.londonpublishingpartnership.co.uk

ISBN: 978-1-907994-14-2 (pbk.)

A catalogue record for this book is
available from the British Library

This book has been composed in Candara

Copy-edited and typeset by
T&T Productions Ltd, London

Cover design: Kate Prentice

Contents

Chapter 1

Introduction

It seems impossible to be neutral about London. Samuel Johnson opined that when one is tired of London, one is tired of life, but William Cobbett described it as a 'great wen' and a 'monster'. These conflicting opinions are still with us, although possibly not so memorably expressed. Both the current mayor of London, Boris Johnson, and his predecessor, Ken Livingstone, have described it as the greatest city on earth, but perhaps they would say that. Their opinions of their city differ much less than their politics.

Other views have not always been so positive. Professor Roy Porter published a social history of London in 1994. It ends on a note of pessimism about London's prospects, fearing that the city might become a museum piece. It was just as well he also pointed out that historians make poor forecasters, as London was even then on the cusp of its own reinvention.

His last paragraph ends: 'London is a muddle that works. Will it stay that way?' The answer would appear to be yes. London and Londoners have rethought their city, its governance and its geography. Only the Rolling Stones appear to be the exception to the rule that change is constant. All great cities need to change. This book looks at how London has been reinvented in the past, and describes the reinvention it is experiencing now. It also asks what is necessary to ensure that this wave of change succeeds and that London continues to prosper.

I grew up in the outer suburbs, in what used to be called the commuter belt, and I went to school in London in the 1960s, travelling by train and spending winter afternoons warming myself on the coal fire in Surbiton station's art deco waiting room. I gave in to teachers who said I would be foolish to aim to be a geologist, since women were not allowed on oil rigs and oil was the future for geologists. I went as a teenager to London to gawp at Biba and Mary Quant but couldn't afford any of the clothes. I made most of my wardrobe on the old Singer sewing machine at home, with designer patterns, trying to live up to the new times. Air conditioning was unheard of, and so were daily showers. Central heating was rare.

It is important to remind ourselves from time to time about how enormously lifestyles have changed for the better over these past fifty years – change enabled by economic growth and higher incomes. The reinvention of our capital city and its surrounding hinterland has been a crucial part of that change. In the 1970s it was hard to imagine the London of the new millennium. It seemed as if London, and indeed the United Kingdom, was struggling. Successive oil crises in 1974 and 1979 exacerbated the decline of industries saddled with complacent management and disgruntled workforces. London was losing population and losing jobs. The new towns planned around the edge of the city, such as Basingstoke, Stevenage, Harlow and Milton Keynes, seemed destined to be the sources of growth. The swinging sixties had touched far too small a part of London to make more than a small dent in the general feeling of doom and gloom. Yet change did come. In 2002, when I became the first chief economist to the newly formed Greater London Authority (GLA), my initial task was to prepare long-term projections for the city as the basis for a new London

Plan. Those forecasts showed expected employment growth of 435,000 between 2001 and 2011, a scale of job creation sceptics said could not be achieved. In the event, 427,000 additional jobs were created. I am glad I stuck to my guns.

The general thrust of my projections did not change over the following ten years and they continued to be largely accurate. London has even bounced back from the recent post-crisis recession. In the summer of 2013, employment was higher than at the previous peak in 2008, and output was back to 99 per cent of the peak. Short-term indicators are all positive. The doom-mongers of 2008, when Lehman Brothers collapsed, appear to have been mistaken, at least as far as London is concerned. The latest projections from the GLA (not now my responsibility) suggest that, if anything, employment growth has accelerated. Population is now expected to increase by 1.7 million and employment by 850,000 by 2036. The challenge is to provide the conditions in which these projections can be successfully realized, through a further reinvention of London's economy.

How can this be brought about? Successful urban reinvention depends on changing, in the right way, four interrelated elements of the economy. These are

- the structure of output and employment, enabling new activities and jobs to be created;
- the places people live and the kind of people moving into London, through appropriate planning and building, ensuring there is a suitable workforce;
- transport links and other infrastructure, so that people can get around easily; and
- communications, especially international connections, so that trade can continue to grow, London being quintessentially a trading city.

The rest of this book looks at each element in turn, at the past and at the scope for the next reinvention. In each case, I take a particular London location as symbolic of the issues: Docklands, Croydon, King's Cross and Heathrow.

Making and doing: the changing structure of the London economy

London's habit of reinvention is not new. Between 1932 and 1937, 532 new factories were set up in London, 83 per cent of the United Kingdom's total. Many of these were new enterprises, making new kinds of goods. They located along what became the North Circular and out along the new radial trunk roads: the A1 out to Enfield and the North, the A4 to Hounslow and the West, the A3 to Kingston and down to Portsmouth. Places such as Park Royal became home to 250 factories before the outbreak of World War II. These new factories made radios and other electrical goods, as well as cars. Hoovers were manufactured along the A40, light bulbs along the A1 by Osram and Phillips, records by EMI at Hayes in Middlesex. Telephones were produced in Hendon and turbines in Wembley. Cosmetics were produced on the Kingston bypass. Food and drink production also became more mechanized and took place on a larger scale, with Lyons Bakeries, Guinness and Heinz at Park Royal, while Beechams had a factory on the A4 at Brentford, and Ilford Photographics, established before World War I in (you guessed it) Ilford, expanded its business as consumer demand grew.

All these new industries were consumer oriented. Many of them made it easier for women to work, as the use of electric cookers, toasters and kettles spread (made by women and used by women). Dishwashers came later; I remember my mother insisting that she had to have one when she went back to work in the early 1960s. This was revolution indeed. Clothes washing followed a different trajectory, since commercial laundries had existed for some time and could be replaced by the launderette. Domestic washing machines took longer to penetrate the home. We had a top-loading paddle machine but it didn't spin, and the mangle was a horrid contraption that was hard work and dangerous to the fingers. Even in the 1970s many women continued to use the launderette.

The earnings generated in the new industries in the 1930s made it possible for their workers to buy the new houses springing up along the suburban rail lines out to the north-west of the capital, or those served by burgeoning bus systems. In one decade, between 1921 and 1931, the outer suburbs attracted 810,000 people, and another 900,000 arrived in the following eight years as London attracted people trying to escape the depressed North, Scotland and Wales. New goods created new markets and new jobs and attracted new people. It is said that the building boom of the 1930s helped rescue London from depression. It would be truer to say that new inventions and the arrival of new firms and much foreign direct investment made the building boom possible. People bought the houses.

The war put all this on hold. Its aftermath saw resources being put into rebuilding, and into new town centres and planning. Spatial expansion was limited by Green Belts. Still, the factories continued to operate, if rather less effectively. It was only in the 1970s that they began to close. I remember the cosmetics factory along the A3 still operating in the 1960s. I visited radio factories and lamp factories in north London as late as the 1980s. None remain now. These sites are sometimes empty, but it is more likely that they have been redeveloped for housing or retail. The Hoover factory in Perivale, listed for its glorious art deco façade, is now a mixture of offices and a Tesco supermarket.

In its post-war reinvention, London recentralized. Pre-war, suburban sprawl and London County Council rehousing reduced urban density across the city. This in turn led to the Abercrombie plans, produced after the war but fundamentally based on a pre-Blitz view of London as a growth problem that needed to be stopped. People and jobs had to be moved out and ring roads were needed to move people round. Fortunately for London, Abercrombie's most draconian visions were never accepted, since they would have involved complete clearing of many areas to provide for more 'rational' segregation of people and activities, as well as restrictions on the heights of buildings. He was more successful in cities such as Plymouth, completing the destruction started by bombing and ripping out the medieval street plan still more effectively. That city has not recovered. However, a mix of planning constraints, Green Belts and war weariness did manage to stop London's growth in its tracks after at least a century of expansion. It took until the mid 1980s for it to get going again.

Or rather, it took until then for people to notice what was happening. It had become fashionable in the 1980s to talk about the economy as one of 'market towns'. Out-of-town centres, retail hubs and office parks were all the rage, and we all travelled by car. Even though there had been two oil price crises – one of which meant that the government went as far as issuing petrol ration books (I still have mine, as well as my childhood one, which I can only just remember, for chocolate) – the car, and the personal freedom it enabled, was key. The first thing I wanted to do on my seventeenth birthday was to get behind a steering wheel. And this perception remained even while the world was actually changing. Business services has been on a pretty constant upward trend for decades, even while other activities were declining (Figure 1.1). This kind of employment is largely office work, where meetings and the need for contact with one another hold sway. It is all much easier in the city centre, and so this has been the latest shift in employment.

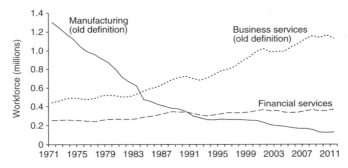

Figure 1.1. Employment chart showing the shift from manufacturing.

In 1971, there were more than a million jobs in manufacturing in London. The latest estimates, for 2012, show that there are fewer than 200,000 left (according to this definition). In 1971, there were around 400,000 jobs in business-to-business services. There are now about a million. We have succeeded in replacing all those jobs lost in declining manufacturing industries with many more jobs, but in different kinds of roles involving different kinds of goods and services. On the other hand, it might come as a surprise to see that the number of people working in finance and insurance has not changed much over the same period: it is still roughly 350,000.

The reinvention of work continues, both along the current trajectory and potentially into new possibilities. Chapter 2 examines this further by tracing the redevelopment of Docklands and the rise and fall of financial services. I argue that some aspects of both the rise and the fall are myths, and that they obscure the broader and much more important picture of service industries more generally, in which London is a world leader. The digital age heightens the importance of these strengths and leads to new opportunities in services, entertainment and new products. London should be well placed to exploit these opportunities if we manage to keep our nerve.

Living and localities

After all the destruction during World War II, bomb sites were still colonized by rosebay willowherb decades later; it is not surprising this plant is known as fireweed in the United States. A shortage of offices and the slow return of people to the capital meant that residential buildings in central London had temporary permission for office occupation, much of which has only expired in the last ten years or so. Over the decades, the work has moved from all those suburban factories to office blocks in the centre of the city.

Even so, London remains a low-density, suburban city (Figure 1.2). With roughly the same population and the same land area as Hong Kong, the distribution of people is completely different. Hong Kong has high-rise blocks and unpopulated hills, and dwelling densities as high as 1,250 per hectare. London has miles and miles of terraced streets, and even its employment densities are low.

The City of London has an employment density of around 300,000 people per square mile, and Westminster has one of around 75,000. New York's is up to 600,000 in the midtown core; that of Paris's central business district sits at around 90,000. London can increase this density if it wants to and still remain a city in which it is a pleasure to live.

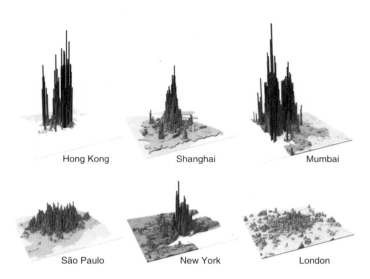

Hong Kong Shanghai Mumbai

São Paulo New York London

Figure 1.2. City density map. (Hong Kong: © Urban Age, LSE Cities, London School of Economics and Political Science. Other five cities: © LSE Cities, London School of Economics and Political Science.)

The most densely populated residential district is Kensington and Chelsea, at 131 people per hectare, though Westminster is at similar levels if the Royal Parks are excluded. Barcelona has up to 400 dwellings per hectare, while the highest dwelling density in London is in Westminster, with 300. This is not about a failure to build high: Barcelona is not a city of tower blocks. Many of London's post-war estates were built at lower population densities than you would find in a series of mansion blocks in Kensington. Various architects have shown that terraced housing at three to four stories can achieve greater density in more comfort than tower blocks. In other words – and perhaps surprisingly – the rows of Victorian terraces, which remain so popular, generate more density than the deeply unpopular high-rise buildings that give high density a bad name.

It is not clear whether the suburban sprawl is due to preference or plan. Planners themselves argued for low-density housing when slums were cleared – as low as twelve houses per acre (120 per hectare) – providing semi-detached houses with gardens to promote healthy living away from overcrowded slums. It would have been cheaper to build terraces, and it is not at all clear why this did not happen. Probably they were not considered 'modern', even if people would have liked them. Solid mansion blocks of flats are popular and, in the right location, now extremely expensive.

However, the built environment is slow to change. Neither Christopher Wren nor Patrick Abercrombie succeeded completely in their grand plans to change the geography of London after conflagrations. Wren managed Regent Street but no other major boulevards, while Abercrombie's ring roads were never completed either, although the Archway road proposal dragged on for a generation.

Although the built environment changes little, the character of the different parts of London and the identity of their inhabitants have changed substantially. Around the turn of the twentieth century, Charles Booth undertook a mammoth survey of life and labour in London. He rated every part of the city. Thus, the parish of All Saints in Knightsbridge beside Hyde Park is rated yellow – 'upper middle and upper classes, wealthy' – in some parts and red – 'middle class, well to do' – in others. We would probably rate it similarly today, though perhaps more coyly. Booth's bottom rating is black – 'lowest class, vicious, semi-criminal'. This category is given to some locations in the parish of All Hallows in Bow, for example. I doubt that Experian or CACI, who provide detailed categorization of locations for consumer companies, would use such terms. But we know that many of these parts of London remain poor and deprived.

Some places have changed dramatically, though. Spitalfields is an area marked firmly black by Booth. It does not feel vicious and semi-criminal now, with its galleries, boutiques and clubs. On the other hand, it is a stone's throw from Brick Lane, which seems to have been much more industrial when Booth was working, and is now a centre for Bangladeshi food and restaurants, having hosted a whole series of immigrant communities. Spitalfields was a centre of weaving, especially silk, in the seventeenth century when Huguenot refugees settled there. The large windows needed by weavers are still apparent in some of the streets. More recently, Jewish refugees arrived here, and then, post-war, those from the Indian subcontinent.

Waves of immigration are nothing new, and new arrivals tend to start out in poorer places, close to their point of entry. Once they begin to do better, they usually move to better locations with larger, nicer houses. And then the next wave arrives. There has been some speculation about whether this upward movement has halted, but it may rather be that settlement takes time. Somali populations, for example, have existed in London for generations, based around seafaring and living near the docks. More recent influxes have resulted from the civil war but have gravitated to the same areas, though there is also a community to the west in Ealing. Some of these clusters are hard to understand or predict. The centre of Korean London life is in New Malden, near Kingston, but how this was seeded no one seems to know.

An alternative example is Notting Hill. In the 1960s and 1970s this was an area where unscrupulous landlords forced out tenants who had protected rights, to replace them with West Indian immigrants who struggled otherwise to find housing and who could be charged more for smaller flats. One such landlord, Peter Rachman, gave his name to this activity, although his notoriety was more to do with his mistresses, Christine Keeler and Mandy Rice-Davies, and their involvement in the Profumo affair than with his business activities.

Thus, Notting Hill went downhill and became crowded, underprovided with services and poor. It also generated a carnival to reflect its new ethnic identity. However, although the carnival still takes place, the ethnic mix is utterly different. Notting Hill has gentrified. Its proximity to White City, for the BBC (at least until 2013 when the BBC moved back into Portland Place in London), and its ease of access to central London, plus the potential for refurbishing large houses back from multiple-occupation, created the potential for gentrification. So Notting Hill, poor but respectable in Charles Booth's day, has gone both downhill and uphill since then. I think we would now have to characterize it as wealthy.

London is, therefore, not a stable city: people move and groups move, much as the West Indians disappeared from Notting Hill, although to where I don't know. It is also a city of suburbs; it is a typical conceit that we should welcome Henry James's description of London as a city of villages. It would be truer, but less romantic, to say it is a city of suburbs. Nowhere better illustrates this history than Croydon. Once a village, it is now well and truly within London, and has suffered the vicissitudes of successive waves of development, of planning and of replanning. In Chapter 3, I look at the future of living in London with reference to this quintessential suburb.

Getting about

The West Indians who moved out of Notting Hill are almost certainly travelling further across the city now than they did then, though they probably do not spend any longer travelling than before. Transport is the glue that holds any city together, along with drains and fuel. No city can survive if its citizens keep dying of bad water, nor if they cannot keep their homes warm and lit. And a city is about moving about. It is salutary to remember that Shanks's pony – walking – remained a primary method of transport in the city until very recently. Read Samuel Pepys's diary and you will find him often walking out to Greenwich to investigate the ships being built before walking home again. Read Trollope's nineteenth-century novels about London and you will find that people walk everywhere, down to the Houses of Parliament, back to Mayfair, and then off again to the City. And of course there was very little option. Roads were narrow and crowded, coaches would be slow. The horse was the only alternative to one's feet.

The horse created its own problems. Like many girls in my time, I cried over the death of Ginger in *Black Beauty*, worked to death in the shafts of a hansom cab. Horses had to be stabled, manure carted, feed and water provided; they are powerful but not simple animals. The horse limited the size of the city. So too did disease. In the medieval period the lure of the city was strong, because the rewards were high. But so were the risks, and the city needed continuous replenishment from the country because death rates were so high. By the twentieth century better drains reduced these risks, though in fact the source of cholera was not understood until late in the nineteenth century. Fortunately, dealing with the stink of bad water dealt with the water quality, even though it was the stink that was thought to be the problem. It is extraordinary that between Roman times and our own so little thought was given to the very basic issue of effluent and drains.

The city was transformed not only by drains but also by the combination of rail, buses and electricity. Horse-drawn bus services made commuting possible even before the dawn of the train. Omnibuses – for all – first brought workers from Paddington to the City from 1829. George Shillibeer's buses gave clerks and smaller merchants the opportunity to live further away from the city, improve their quality of life and enlarge the space they could afford. No change there then.

By 1900, Shillibeer's successor, the London General Omnibus Company, owned nearly half the capital's 3,000 horse-drawn buses and trams, carrying some 5 million passengers a year. Buses could get into the centre of London and carried higher earners, while trams ended at the city fringes and were for working men, who started work earlier than those in the buses.

However, it is the train that we have to thank for the geography of most of London today. It is not too much of a stretch to contend that the train was the key invention that made the industrial revolution a worldwide phenomenon. It made it possible to connect cities and countries in an utterly different way, and to transport goods more widely and more easily than ever before. People were latecomers to train use – most lines were originally built for freight – but from the 1830s on, the commuter railway made possible the outer suburbs, and subsequently the Underground connected all the railway termini and the inner suburbs in new ways too.

The year 2013 marked 150 years of the Underground in London. Compared with now, in 1863 the Underground was not a very pleasant experience. The trains were pulled by steam engines and the coaches had no lighting systems. Electric lighting systems were only introduced in the 1880s and the first Act of Parliament to control this was passed in 1882, with the first power station built in Deptford in 1891. Electrification of the transport system came later, with electric trams appearing in Hammersmith in 1901, running from Shepherd's Bush to Acton. The Lots Road power station became operational in 1905 to power the Piccadilly line – following a construction period that only started in 1901. It is hard to imagine how quickly things were both planned and built in this period.

The London Underground had a second power station at Greenwich but that has since closed, with the system now supplied through the National Grid. Electric trams and electric trains changed the face of the city, paving the way for the retirement of the horse, and making possible the Clean Air Act in due course after the war. However, power stations initially meant coal and smoke. At least eighteen power stations have been constructed in London over the years. The earliest, in Deptford, Woolwich, Shoreditch, Croydon and Kingston, were developed to provide lighting, while the next tranche – in Barking, Brimsdown, Neasden and West Ham – powered trams and the new Underground. The biggest expansion was in the Edwardian period, with stations at Greenwich, Hackney, Kingston, Stepney and Taylor's Lane, Willesden. These were all coal fired and are all now closed, though newer gas-fired stations operate at Taylors Lane and Brimsdown (Enfield). Newer stations appeared during the 1930s and 1940s at Bankside, Battersea and Brunswick Wharf, while Bulls Bridge in Hayes appeared as a gas-fired site in the 1970s. All have since closed. Bankside is now the Tate Modern art gallery, while Battersea is a listed structure still seeking love and attention (and investment). The others have been swept away completely. Power generation in London still happens in Barking (at a gas-fired site), Enfield, Croydon (also at a gas-fired site some half a mile from the original station, where one remaining chimney now marks the IKEA store), and at the Combined Heat and Power incinerator in Bermondsey. Greenwich remains as back-up capacity.

Power, transport and public health are the core infrastructure for any city, as the Romans perhaps knew better than we do. They founded London where it is because Southwark is the easiest place to cross the Thames when arriving from the south. However, London was abandoned when the Romans left. Its stone buildings would have fallen into disrepair and the city would have been a frightening place. Certainly the Saxons did not want it: they formed a settlement just up river and called it Lundenwic. It was used as a trading post and possibly not even regularly settled. Aldwych is the old market and part of the Saxon town. The Fleet River marked the boundary between the two cities and, over succeeding centuries, it remained the demarcation between the trading city, run by its aldermen in the City of London, and the administrative city in Westminster. The Fleet River became the drain for both and a huge risk to public health.

The ability for people to move around safely is essential to the well-being of a city, as is the creation of a healthy environment. In Chapter 4, I use the redevelopment of King's Cross and St Pancras as an example of how transport improvements and public realm investment can change a location and generate economic growth as well. Transport may not be sufficient to generate growth, but it is certainly necessary.

The international dimension

There is a comic song (by Michael Flanders) that explains the laws of thermodynamics, the refrain of which goes:

> 'You can't pass heat from a cooler to a hotter,
> You can try it if you like but you'd far better notter
> Cos the cold from the cooler will get hotter as a ruler,
> and that's a physical law!'

I have always found this useful in remembering the second law of thermodynamics, but I wish that there was anything half so clear in economics. I have spent a considerable proportion of my career trying to develop models and results that do not depend on incorrect assumptions or on a belief that using the word 'perfect' in a description means that such a world would be either desirable or achievable. In the process of considering how economic analysis actually works, however, one thing stands out as a rule: trade creates growth. Trade makes it possible to divide labour, exploit scale, use raw materials and transfer knowledge. The benefits of trade may not always be distributed as we would wish, but they are always there.

Trade can, of course, happen at many levels – between individuals, between communities and regions, and between countries. International trade has been a feature of all wealthy civilizations. The ancient Greeks decorated their temples with colour from Asia, the Mediterranean and the Caucasus. Rome traded across its known world. The discovery of the Americas opened up new trade opportunities and created what is currently the world's richest country. China, on the other hand, closed its borders for several centuries and lost its technological advantage. It is now catching up. The inter-war period saw a diminution of trade, reflecting growing protectionism of home industry and jobs. This reduced employment and prosperity rather than increasing it, however. Trade shifts activity and employment, but this can be part of what Schumpeter called the waves of creative destruction. London's jobs are centred where trade happens: central London, Heathrow, Docklands and around subsidiary centres such as Croydon (Figure 1.3).

Technology can drive such waves of restructuring. This could be the technology that harnessed steam power, that which produced electric motors, or cars, or it could be the

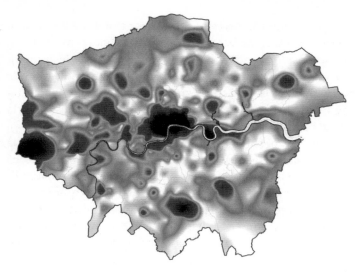

Figure 1.3. London employment density map, 2003. Darker colours are areas of higher employment density. (© Greater London Authority.)

technology now giving us cloud computing, and which enables me to research this book almost entirely while sitting at my laptop.

London has always been a fulcrum in Britain's trade with the world. Though the west coast ports of Bristol and Liverpool grew rich on trade with the Americas, London was still participating. Bristol had the slave trade, but more slaves were traded in London, just less obviously. Whether with ships or aeroplanes or via the airwaves, London trades. The meridian line at Greenwich does not of itself put London at the centre of the world's time zones, but merely reflects London's importance in trading relationships when those zones were established in 1851. But the time zones still reflect reality. New York is five hours behind, Delhi five hours ahead. London is the location where working hours in all these zones overlap.

This is a huge advantage, as is the global use of English as a business language.

However, to be a centre of world trade, communication of all kinds must function effectively. I will examine this in relation to our love–hate relationship with Heathrow, to aviation and to our policymaking mechanisms in Chapter 5.

Chapter 2

Finance and other services: Docklands

London's Docklands, dominated by the towers of Canary Wharf, stand as a symbol of the role of financial services in the capital's economy – a role called into question by the impact of the 2008 financial crisis. But Docklands also symbolizes past shifts in the structure of London's economy. If such large shifts have occurred before, they can do so again. Financial services are not as dominant as many people imagine, and form only one aspect of London's broader strength in services. This latest crisis does not spell doom for London's service-focused economy.

The London docks were once the centre of the world's physical trade. The centre of the globe's largest empire saw all sorts of goods come through its docks, which spread downriver on both banks from the wharves by London Bridge. Five docks were opened in the early years of the twentieth century, with the final and largest dock, the King George V, completed as late as 1921. By the mid 1930s the docks were at their peak (Figure 2.1). More than 35 million tonnes of cargo passed through the docks each year, carried by 55,000 ship movements and served by more than 10,000 lighters. In all, some 100,000 men were dependent on the Port of London for employment, more than 30,000 of whom were employed by the port itself.

However, by the early 1980s, only fifty years later, the Port of London Authority employed only 3,000 people and almost all the docks had closed. A huge area of London appeared to be derelict. This cautionary tale is important to all industries that appear to be dominant, and reflects the rapidity with which change can take hold. The decline of the dock trade was down to a variety of factors, with complacency perhaps being a key one. The new technology of containerization, combined with larger ships, could not be supported in older docks, while the labour force strongly resisted any change. The wartime National Dock Labour Scheme effectively protected the right to be a docker and limited competition. Management failed to grasp this nettle and trade was diverted to newer ports. Much

Figure 2.1. Historic photograph of Canary Wharf.
Courtesy of the PLA Collection (Museum of London).

large-scale trade went to the Netherlands and Germany, with only smaller ships making the trip across the channel.

Regeneration efforts for Docklands started almost as soon as the docks closed, and the London Docklands Development Corporation (the major redevelopment body) was set up in 1981 by Michael Heseltine, then secretary of state for the environment, with the previous ten years having been spent on various planning discussions and debates. At this point, no one had a plan for the Docklands to become a major financial or business centre. The main options had been to develop housing of different sorts, with various mixes of commercial and industrial uses.

Several interrelated factors drove Docklands in a different direction. Much like the interaction of technology, regulation, policy and timing that culminated in the docks' closure, similar interaction drove their reconfiguration. The technological change was the rise of new communication and computer technologies, which were revolutionizing trade in services just as containers had revolutionized trade in goods. This change was driving a need for larger floorplates and more room for cabling. The regulatory change was the 'Big Bang': a removal of restrictions on organizations within the City that had prevented them scaling up. The regulatory restriction that remained was the planning regime in the City itself, which made it hard to develop the new larger buildings that new larger companies needed to house the new technologies. The 'Big Bang' for Docklands was the product of the imagination of a pair of Canadians, the Reichman brothers, who saw this area as an opportunity to provide the kind of buildings that were needed, if only the transport could keep pace. The other accident of timing was the willingness of the then prime minister, Margaret Thatcher, to override the normal processes of decision making for transport schemes. The extension of the

Underground to this new business centre would be crucial to the massive buildings envisaged by the Reichman brothers (Figure 2.2). The Docklands Light Railway, planned to provide local links to small-scale industry, would not provide anything like the necessary capacity, nor the necessary connections into the heart of London. But the Jubilee Line Extension did not pass any of the tests necessary to justify the investment. Only a political decision could override this.

Figure 2.2. Canary Wharf viewed from the Shard.
Courtesy of Christopher Rosewell.

This combination of events led to the development of a new financial centre, well to the east of the existing financial concentration. And, in response, the City itself changed its planning policies to facilitate the kind of buildings and densities favoured by city firms. The race to build taller buildings is still going on. In Docklands, skyscrapers are rising in Wood Wharf, while on the south side of London Bridge, the Shard is pushing city activities and densities into Southwark, and in the City itself various other nicknamed buildings have emerged: the Gherkin, the Walkie-Talkie and the Cheese-grater. All of these have more normal addresses but are much better known by their monikers.

This description sounds like a regulatory and planning free-for-all, a neocon response to a political environment. It is important to appreciate that the truth is much more complicated, especially if we are to understand the more recent history and where Docklands, and London business generally, might go next.

The regulatory changes were not happening in a vacuum, still less in a stable environment. They were themselves a response to a changing environment. Just as dockers failed to withstand the tide of containerization, so too traditional broking failed to withstand the tide of computerization. Computers in financial services started as record keepers, producing statements and validating trades. But even while the systems that produced bank statements in the 1970s were being written, the opportunities to manage information as well as records were being developed.

All such opportunities could increase the scale of organizations and the amount of business they could undertake – as well as their geographical spread, as computer speeds changed the speed of data communication. In 1970 I had a job checking the output of a computer against the accounting machines recording the trades of a pension fund. The computer usually got it wrong. Forty years later when the system failed for just one day at RBS and its subsidiaries, there was outrage, and significant transactions teetered on the brink of failure. This technological shift changed the economic geography of the city.

It also changed the economic description of the labour force in equally complex ways. Jobs in the docks, hard manual labour, were not replaced by jobs for stockbrokers and city grandees with long lunches and chauffeurs. Indeed, there has not been much change in the numbers employed in city-type sectors in this period. But it is not only the skills of these people that have changed dramatically, it is the whole ecosystem that runs alongside them. The typical denizen of Docklands, and the City of London, is a graduate, often with a technical degree. They are familiar with a raft of regulations, and with the pricing and margins of many products. They work long hours and have lunch at their desk. A visit to some major offices would make you think of a wage slave rather than a grandee. The days of panelled offices and large desks are more a memory than the reality.

Most people working in the 'City', whether in central London or in Docklands, do not work in any kind of bank. And though financial and other kinds of services are not manual industries, as dock work is, they are both intermediation and service trades. Dockers enabled the transition of goods from ship to shore or vice versa. They neither made the goods nor the ships. Dock work is just as much a service as organizing the insurance for the goods or lending the money to buy a ship.

This raises a crucial question for modern economies: the source of value. It somehow seems intuitively right that bankers and finance specialists create nothing. It has equally been argued that advertising creates nothing and that management consultants are a way of telling you what you already know – and, of course, lawyers and accountants are well known to be an incubus on all and sundry.

Economic value

What is economic value? It is not just about making things, since we clearly need and want services as well. The calculation of 'output' or GDP looks at value added, the difference between what is bought in and what is sold. When a woman pays another to do childcare or household chores instead of doing them herself, this increases output. And if by doing this she herself is able to add more value than she pays her nanny, the net gain is clear.

If she is selling her services to foreigners who bring in foreign resources to pay her, then this definitively increases the net resources available to the inhabitants of our country. External trade is good. But any form of market can be good if it increases the ability to raise productivity, exploit economies of scale or the division of labour.

But of course a lot depends on the price. If the power relationships mean that the net benefit of my going to work and paying someone else to look after my children is expropriated by my employer (or if it nearly is), then I am only marginally better off. If I sell my services to foreigners who will only pay me a low price – arguing, no doubt, that there is a lot of international competition – then my gains of trade will be small in relation to theirs. Power cannot be separated from the operation of markets and it shifts all the time.

The United Kingdom earns much of its foreign exchange with services of one kind or another. Whether it is banking, insurance, computer services or marketing, these are all industries in which we have world-leading firms, most of which are based in London. These are both specialisms and areas of international expertise. Advertising agencies, sellers of international swaps and international dispute-mediation services are bringing in financial support for the rest of the country as surely as selling rails and a locomotive to run on them were in earlier years. We should celebrate all of them.

So long as the price is fair. The concept of the fair or just price has a long pedigree. Too high a price and no one buys and trade makes no gains. But too low a price and all the gain goes to others. Long ago David Ricardo described how trade may make us all better off. By making more of the things that I produce better than you, while you make more of the things that you produce better than me, we may both be richer. How much richer depends on how we divide the spoils, a subject on which economists are generally silent. We only require that you should be richer to the extent that you would choose to engage in trade in the first place. Normal people, on the other hand, care deeply about fairness. A moral case can be made against economics for undermining that sense of fairness, for teaching that something is always better than nothing. A society that runs on respect and that thinks it is right to offer a half share might be a better place to live and a more secure place to do business. London might become a sink of iniquity if the economists were allowed to be in charge, understanding the price of everything but the value of nothing.

All of this shows that we should not frown on service industries, and especially not on those that earn foreign exchange. But we might frown on those that capture too large a share of the gains from trade, or that capture the gains of others. This is the origin of our unease about financial services: that while they are a source of conspicuous consumption, we are unable to understand how such activity can be so valuable.

This discussion sheds light on why so many people believe that the financial crisis has caused lasting damage to London. Unfortunately, the financial crisis can only be partly blamed on spiv traders. Most bankers are not traders, and most believed throughout that extending lending was about meeting peoples' needs. A collective illusion emerged that risk was a thing of the past and could be managed away. On top of this, low interest rates and low inflation meant that investors such as pension funds chased returns on behalf of their pensioners, while borrowers believed there could be an end to boom and bust. Those warning that the risk of a recession was much higher than the zeitgeist suggested were told they were wrong: told by the Bank of England, by eminent journalists and by the regulators. I know this because that is what happened to a paper written by me to consider the successes of the Bank of England's Monetary Policy Committee. That paper, first written in 2005, praised the introduction of 'fan charts', which display a range of potential outcomes for the economy and for inflation, but argued that they were far too narrow and that the risk of recession was a positive one. At the height of the boom, however, no one cared.

One lesson to be taken from this is that there is always boom and bust and risks are always with us. The economists' models suggesting otherwise were wrong. Bankers and borrowers who believed this hype were wrong. But banking and borrowing are essential to an economy, even when risky. Savers want to get a return to build a pension pot. Borrowers want to finance firms, or mortgages or inventions. Without banks, you can only invest your own resources, and individual risk skyrockets. Unfortunately, there is no such thing as a utility bank that takes no risk. It is inherent in banking and is paid for in the gap between lending and borrowing rates. This gap – essential to cover risk and costs – is the heart of the problem. In 2006, sitting on the board of a building society, I debated with my colleagues how we could continue to lend when competition had pushed borrowers' rates below those at which we could attract funds. What was the minimum level of business that we could do and still stay in action?

The other part of the finance story is arbitrage. At one level this is just about efficiency, moving things or capital to where they attract better prices is a good way to grasp the benefits of opportunities. Silicon Valley entrepreneurs do this all the time. However, when arbitrage becomes the main focus of finance, the lunatics (admittedly very clever lunatics) are in charge of the asylum. A toxic combination of optimism about continued borrowing and cleverness in arbitrage is at the root of the crisis. As ever with a major event, there is no single simple cause. If there were, it would be easy to find and to fix, even in advance. Not all bankers are venal, not all regulators were asleep at the wheel, not all traders are greedy and amoral. Nobody denies that the system failed to control those without moral standards. Both weeding out those for whom greed is the only good and setting standards of behaviour inside institutions offer better protection for consumers than any amount of regulation. I am an SIF – a new acronym for a 'significant influence function' – as a director of Ulster Bank. Sessions for persons in these functions now include consideration of knotty ethical questions about dealmaking, bidding for work and so on. They are not just about what the regulator wants. 'My word is my bond' is returning as the motto of the City.

Financial services remain essential to the development of trade, to structuring deals, to managing savings. London's ability to be at the centre of this in a world where the balance of international trade is shifting remains important not only to its ability to earn foreign exchange but also to its ability to finance new and innovative companies in the United Kingdom.

Of course, the City is no longer the geographical hub of finance that it was. An incidental but crucial impact of the redevelopment of Docklands was on the planning policies of the City of London, which reacted to the competition by loosening rules on tall buildings and footplate size. Most of these new buildings are occupied by lawyers, accountants and other business services. Bankers are not in fact especially prevalent.

At the heart of London, from the West End to Docklands, are high-density connected businesses. This is an agglomeration – a term that gives a sense of stickiness, of how things work together. When the whole is greater than the sum of the parts, productivity of each part is enhanced. We will come back to this in the next section. In the meantime, this chapter has shown that financial services and banking are not inherently bad, and indeed they are necessary. We should not throw the financial baby out with the bathwater of too much debt.

Neither is finance the only game in town. Docklands and the City are already home to far more than traders and bankers. They house world-class companies across law, accounting, marketing, engineering, architecture and design: a wide-ranging economic sector known as business services. Such businesses employ the vast majority of people employed in London. The bank HSBC employs 8,000 in London and 85,000 worldwide, while the accountants and consultants PwC employ 180,000 across the globe and also have 8,000 staff in London.

Tech city

What are business services? This is a category which is itself morphing. Google, the construction of whose London headquarters in King's Cross is due to be completed in 2016, clearly offers services to businesses, charging them for click-throughs. But it is not a business service in the standard way. Playgen is a company that designs games and simulations used by other businesses – they are a cross between management consultants and games designers – and their office is located in Spitalfields. A map exists of a so-called Tech City that has emerged around the rather ugly roundabout at Old Street station, now renamed Silicon Roundabout. This set of businesses on the edge of the City itself, in an area of cheap business property, may eventually be pulled west towards Google's UK headquarters in King's Cross or east towards the Olympic Park, or it may develop its own new premises as it gets successful and grows. It will not stand still.

Business services will go on developing and morphing and changing their geography at the same time. The bright young quants who were attracted to financial services and its excitement, which is always at least as important as financial reward, especially at the start of a career, are now looking for jobs in rather different sorts of firm. They may look different from the outside, but inside they will offer the same heady mix of innovation, hard work and potential reward that investment banks once did.

London's continued and continuing ability to reinvent itself relies on its ability to attract bright young things who are well educated and ambitious. Alongside this, it matters that there is scope to reinvent the city's key locations and to create the kind of buzz that is produced by emerging businesses who do not feel hidebound by the past. In May 2013 I attended an event in Shoreditch Town Hall, distinctly on the fringe of the City. It was entitled Digital Shoreditch and celebrated the emerging businesses that are focused there, just down the road from the Old Street roundabout. The event's location encapsulates the process of reinvention. Shoreditch Town Hall is a High-Victorian edifice, with big staircases and a first-floor hall that has no doubt seen a huge variety of public meetings. After its first redundancy, when Shoreditch merged with Hackney and Stoke Newington during local government reorganization in the 1960s, it became the home of boxing matches. Now it hosts entrepreneurs and geeks. It is no stranger to technical innovation either, since it was from here that Shoreditch managed its earliest electric lighting plants, located nearby, and which are now themselves performance spaces, near the achingly trendy Hoxton Square.

What value is being created here? Could this just be another buzzy phase that doesn't really lead anywhere, like the swinging sixties? Actually, perhaps that statement warrants some reassessment. At Glastonbury in 2013, the Rolling Stones showed, by all accounts, that the sixties produced some of the country's most enduring music, able to stand the test of time. This same year, there was an exhibition of David Bowie's work at the Victoria and Albert Museum. The sixties explosion of creativity, music and designers such as Paul Smith, Terence Conran and Mary Quant set the parameters for energy and enterprise across the city in other fields too. I recently went to a private view of the David Bowie exhibition, sponsored by a major accountancy firm. It was instructive to see how many of the business people there, active in fields across all sectors, had been inspired by Bowie and were in that same age group. The activities themselves have earned the United Kingdom considerable foreign earnings over the years, even if the traditional music industry has struggled to adapt to the digital age.

Tech City and its relatives are operating in that digital age. Some of the energy of this emerging sector will create new forms of entertainment, new games, new methods of storytelling. But much of it will feed back into the advertising industry, marketing, product design and product definition. There is huge scope for the kind of invention London can be good at. The part of the Digital Shoreditch event that I went to was called Nudgestock and was sponsored by Ogilvy and Mather. Speakers included Nassim Taleb (once a fund manager and now the author of a series of books, including one entitled *Black Swan*) and a senior researcher from Goldman Sachs, as well as my colleague Paul Ormerod, talking about the impact of networks on economic choice.

It always takes time for statistics to catch up with new categories, so we do not have a digital economy measure. However, the Greater London Authority expects professional, scientific and technical activities to be the fastest-growing sector, followed by information and communications activities, while financial and insurance activities are projected to shrink. While financial intermediation employed 144,000 people in 2011, computer consultancy employed 80,000, and programming employed 29,000. Moreover, lawyers, accountants and management consultants accounted for 258,000 jobs. The information and communications sector is expected to become larger than finance and insurance in the next few years.

London can, therefore, continue to grow its economy in this wide range of services, from finance to technology, but will it be the kind of city in which the people that are needed for these high-skill businesses to thrive will want to live? The next chapter looks at living in London.

Chapter 3

Living in London: the suburbs and Croydon

The link between work and housing, between domestic leisure and outside entertainment, is a complicated but important one. Housing quality and a good sewerage system matter a lot, but they do not create a city's atmosphere. The character of the places available for people to live is a vital factor in economic success – and in London that means thriving suburbs.

Where the weather is warm, interior and exterior lives merge, from café society to women on their doorsteps watching the world go by. In northern latitudes this has turned into pub culture for men and scrubbing the doorstep for women, with clubs and societies mediating between the two; at least that is the traditional view. Growing up in 1950s suburbia was not quite so stereotypical but it certainly shared some clear views on gender roles and behaviours. Women mostly did not work and men expected to be looked after. Much has changed since then, but suburbia still sits somewhere between village life, where everything is known and judged, and the anonymity of the city. In suburbia, one still suspects that disapproval awaits whoever steps out of line. Which might be why I did, of course. By then it was the 1960s though and my mother, to her credit, was happy for me to go on the pill – so long as I went to a clinic in the next town rather than the one next door to our house. It was a pity, and remains one of my life's most embarrassing memories, that when I got there the doctor turned out to be a family friend.

The localism inherent in these kinds of links is sometimes sneered at. Suburban living gets a bad press, yet the suburbs remain not only where most people live but where they want to live. Croydon epitomizes this tension. In the 1960s, Croydon was designated for growth. It was given roads and underpasses, and office blocks and housing were built as part of the plan to decentralize London. Postcards were printed to advertise the modern living possible in this new town only twenty minutes from central London (Figure 3.1).

Figure 3.1. A 1950s postcard of Croydon Underpass.

The reality has been different. No major private-sector employers remain in Croydon, with Nestlé being the last to move out in 2012. The office blocks are occupied by the likes of the Home Office and the Borders Agency – Croydon is where you need to go to get your residence permit. It is not an attractive destination, with low-budget stores and a shabby air; it was my daughter who described the 'Croydon facelift' achieved by tying your hair back so hard that it tightens the skin. Attempts to change Croydon's image have been acrimonious, dogged by financial problems, and remain unfulfilled. In 2007 I took part in a major planning battle in Croydon. The local council wanted to develop an arena, a smaller version of the O_2, that would host both sporting and music events, and intended to exploit the rail network to central London as well as the tram connections both east and west. The vision was to transform Croydon's image from cheap and downmarket to busy and bustling.

Planning and planners

The arena proposal was established in an effort to change Croydon's image and to bring visitors into a revitalized town centre, where an earlier proposal to redevelop the central shopping centre had already foundered and where the local department store stood empty.

On the other side of the argument stood an experienced developer of office parks. They could point to success in a variety of locations, most recently Chiswick Park, where a bus depot and factory had been redeveloped into a modern office campus. Their vision was that the site, next to East Croydon station, could become just such an office-based development, including some new housing, revitalizing the employment prospects for the town and turning it back into a desirable employment location.

The planning battle was fought out on many fronts. The two leading QCs in the property world sat on either side of the room, working out how best to present the various arguments: on economic need, on the parameters for success, on viability, on architecture, on transport and on planning policies.

Behind them seethed the various experts and supporting lawyers. Rooms slowly, and sometimes not so slowly, filled up with paper, with reports, with follow-up material and with detritus of every sort. My task was to present the economic case for the arena. My colleagues and I researched the viability and feasibility of arenas across the country – one of my colleagues saw Guns N' Roses in more places than she might have liked. We looked at the role of visitor attractions in regeneration and how all of this might fit into the pattern of life in Croydon. I was convinced then, and remain convinced, that Croydon needed a grand and original project such as the arena to create a new image for itself. While our piece of the jigsaw of this major planning case was a large one, it was by no means the only piece. Massive documents of architects' drawings and visualizations of how it would look were prepared by both sides, and policy experts debated whether agreed policies were or were not in support of a particular choice, as well as what was legal.

Unless you have experienced a case such as this, it is hard to grasp how much material can be involved – and in what copious variety. The planning inspector has to listen to it all, absorb it, and then prepare a report.

On this occasion, after several weeks of evidence, and months of preparation, the planning inspector declared in favour of the incumbent, the office developer, who already had permission, which counts for a lot in planning terms. But despite permission being granted, the site remains empty. For the recession hit, and while office property in central London remains attractive, this is not the case in suburban locations.

The financial return is just not appealing enough. Who knows, one day something better and more entertaining may be developed. In the meantime, it has been announced that new investors have been found to regenerate the shopping centre. The investors in question are Hammerson, veteran owners of shopping centres across the United Kingdom, and Westfield, who are thought to be aiming for centres on all four sides of London. They already have Westfield White City and Westfield Stratford, so with Croydon under their belts there is only the northern outpost to find.

Their aim will be to create a shopping destination with a large catchment area, and it may be that this will generate enough style and pizzazz to make a real difference to the town. That is the aim at Stratford too, alongside the housing development and some employment activity rolling off the back of the Olympic investment. Such an investment is certainly closer to the arena vision than to the business park, and it brings us back to the question of the role and purpose of the suburbs.

It also brings us to the knotty problem of planning. It is clear that no one is keen on a free-for-all in development. The recent proposal from the government to increase the size of development that any householder is free to make before requiring planning permission has already had to be watered down to at least require consultation with neighbours.

Unfortunately, it is easier to be clear about what planning is against than about what it is for. If planning prevents change, it also prevents the process of reinvention that is the key to a successful location. It is extraordinary how flexible some forms of development are: this helps, but not all buildings can be reused. Victorian and Georgian terraces have had an amazing run (Figure 3.2). Houses built for utterly different domestic technologies and social constructs remain

Figure 3.2. Victorian terraces. Courtesy of Christopher Rosewell.

not only useful but desirable. In 1995 I bought a terraced house in Wandsworth, expecting to own it for a few years. I sold it in 2012, while family life changed around me. It was built in 1885, with deeds that showed a covenant, long since unenforceable, that prevented me from using the house as a boarding house or a gambling establishment: early planning, but by developers trying to ensure that the street was respectable and the houses, therefore, more valuable. I have no idea who occupied it then, but the generation before me were tradesmen, shopkeepers, local workers. By the time I sold it, the street was populated by bankers, meaning more bathrooms and loft conversions. Houses that had been built with outside toilets and that had added Anderson shelters during the war (next door still had theirs when we moved in) now have limestone floors, state-of-the-art kitchens and landscaped gardens. Nonetheless, the houses still work in a fundamental way and are attractive and comfortable to live in.

There was a period when these suburban terraces were unfashionable, though. Houses in Islington that are now in what became the heart of New Labour territory could be bought for a song in the 1960s. Town planners wanted to pull them down and campaigns were fought by locals to save the architecture that now gives style and value to many local areas. What planning seemed to be for in that period was destruction, and the creation of tower blocks that had to be pulled down before the debts on them were paid off (Figure 3.3).

The collapse of Ronan Point in Canning Town raised serious doubts about risk and construction, and the poor quality of maintenance added to the disfavour into which such blocks fell. A combination of construction quality and accommodation quality hit council blocks hard. Even so, in the private sector towers and taller buildings have had a new lease of life. The reinvention of London living has involved the densification of private apartment building. All along the Thames, as business use of river frontages has declined, blocks of flats have emerged instead. Although achieving the river view may involve dangerous leaning out from the balcony, the ceilings may be low and the room sizes small, these blocks are popular. Few modern blocks allow gas to be used, which has been one of the main sources of serious accidents in blocks in the past.

This trend has been little remarked upon. The main focus of attention is the difficulty young people have in affording to get onto the London property ladder at all. I should at this point admit that, from the Victorian terrace, I have downsized to a modern flat, though in a small block of only four stories. In downsizing it has been possible to liberate some capital to help my children. This is an increasing feature of London housing life. Without the bank of mum and dad, finding the deposit is hard. Part of me thinks that this is nothing new. In the days

Figure 3.3. Tower blocks. Courtesy of Christopher Rosewell.

of banking cartels and limited lending, there was a queue to get a mortgage and one way to get to the head of the queue was to have savings and a decent sized deposit. The bank of mum and dad helped there too. At that time too, rising house prices always seemed to be outstripping the ability to save a deposit, and the ability to buy receded in front of one's eyes.

Space invaders

However, what is really different now is the supply pressure. To an extent this is inevitable. Space is something we all want more of as we grow richer. In my childhood, even well-off families thought it was fine for children to share a bedroom. Now, every child needs their own space, their own television, their own computer, and storage for all the peripherals too. Instead of one room being heated and the whole family sitting in front of one television, they are distributed across a centrally heated house, each doing his or her own thing. I was thirty-five before I lived in a centrally heated house, although now it seems inconceivable to be without such heating. Domestic technologies such as these change the way we live and the way in which we use space, and enable us to demand still more space and still more stuff to put in it. Housing shortages will stay with us unless we get poorer and cannot afford the heating or the space and wish to huddle together for warmth. This is a much worse problem than the problem of wealth and the demand for space and a spare bedroom to boot.

An associated element of the desire for space is the economy of storage. We all have so much stuff. The replacement of industrial units with self-storage 'factories' is a phenomenon of the last fifteen years or so, but it is a good metaphor for our changing economy and society. A newly built self-storage place exists out along the A40 on the way to Hangar Lane. It is on the site of a television factory, which I once visited when investigating the accusation that cheap televisions were being 'dumped' on our shores. This now seems quaint. Indeed, the factory itself was quaint. The storage rooms within probably now store old televisions, unused electronics and other consumer items, none of which were made in the United Kingdom.

All of them contribute to our need for space. Though rooms get smaller, our desire for privacy means we need more rooms at the same time. The cost of all this means that we need storage units as well, just to keep our stuff. Though they charge quite substantial rents, it is not as much as it would cost to have a house capable of holding it all. I am not sure what to make of this irony of modern living in cities, nor sure whether this is just a mini-boom in storage facilities that will wear out as people realize that the stuff is not worth keeping or whether it will accelerate as people want to keep more for future generations, with the storage unit becoming the equivalent of the attic of past generations. Reality TV will no doubt eventually catch up with this new phenomenon, and we will have programmes on what you keep in your storage unit and how much it is worth, *Storage Roadshow* perhaps. For all I know, someone is working on the pilot right now.

Apparently, one reason why people fail to invest in loft insulation is the hassle of clearing out the attic. It is being represented as an example of the 'nudge' policy extravaganza that we now have a policy to subsidize attic clearance. It is not at all clear how this is an example of nudge, which is supposed to be about presenting choices in a way that makes it easier to do the 'right' thing. But I suppose it could be an example of how rationality is more complex than economists sometimes suppose.

None of this solves the problem of where a rising population will live, can live or wants to live. As described earlier, London is not a dense city. Even with the recent apartment-block boom, density is not changing much. Beside the Shard (short for Shard of Glass, but now the address of the building itself beside London Bridge station), the developer wants to construct new residential towers, almost as high as the Shard itself, which has seventy-two stories. These will be thin fingers and the top will need to sway in the wind. In New York, in downtown Manhattan, there are numerous residential towers with more than thirty stories. These are blocks with lifts that work and resident concierges. They are not cheap. You would want to leave town in a hurricane.

The London economy has to rest finally on people, as all economies do. People who cannot find somewhere to live will leave. At present, for many people London is one of the world's most attractive cities in which to live. It is considered to be the most tolerant international city, comfortable with its massive range of nationalities and languages. This is probably true for the internationally mobile with incomes and choices. At the other end of the spectrum it is not so attractive. Tension exists in traditional working class areas where traditional jobs are no more and migrants are prepared to work in jobs that are unappealing to the native born. Neither do migrants exhibit the desire for space that local residents do.

This results in an 'affordable housing' conundrum. Economists will generally think that selling or renting housing for below its construction cost makes no sense. It must be wages that are too low. But in fact none of these markets work, or have probably ever worked, as economists think. They all have rules of planning, of fairness and of long-term versus short-term choices that defy standard analysis.

The price of land in London is high, as are construction costs. People on low wages cannot afford high travel costs, so they need to live near their place of work, precisely where the housing costs are likely to be highest. Either the quality of their accommodation must be lower, or their net incomes must be still worse. A comparable conundrum applies to women's participation in the labour force. Costs are high in the city and so we would expect women to want to work. But the costs of childcare and of travel are also expensive, so the net benefit of doing so can be relatively low. In fact, women's participation in the labour market is lower in London than in the rest of the country and relative wages are worse.

Being a working mother in London is to be in a worse position than elsewhere. Although childless women are as likely to work as in the rest of the country, this is not true for mothers in London. Outside London, nearly 70 per cent of mothers with dependent children work, for Inner London mothers the figure is only 45 per cent, where childcare costs are also around 20 per cent higher. Some of this effect is the result of a relatively large presence of ethnic groups for whom it is considered inappropriate for women to work. But it is also the result of fewer opportunities and more competition. Part-time work, generally the preference for women with school-age children, is both less available and less well paid. The presence of people newly arrived in the United Kingdom, perhaps on temporary work visas, increases the competition for retail and catering roles, often available part time. Thus, while median full-time female earnings are about 50 per cent higher in London than elsewhere, part-time earnings are only 17 per cent higher. On top of which childcare and travel costs are high, decreasing the net benefit of working. Even full time, the gender pay gap remains larger than in the rest of the United Kingdom. This is largely because of the top decile of pay, which is predominantly inhabited by men. The top 10 per cent of earners, both male and female, are significantly higher earners in London than elsewhere, but the wage gap for this group is 44 per cent, compared with 23 per cent on average .

This labour market impetus is, in part, a symptom of London's success in attracting people who want to participate in a successful economy. Even post crisis, London's population continues to grow. Leveraging the skills of women into the lower end of the labour market remains a challenge if there is not to be increasing hidden family poverty.

Until recently, I might also have said there was a challenge on the education front. Ten years ago, London's schools were worse than the UK average in delivering both GCSE and A level results. This is no longer true. In spite of the ethnic mix and the inclusion of the most deprived areas in the country, standards have dramatically improved. This is attributed to the advent of academies, Teach First (a scheme to bring young graduates into education) and free schools, as well as to the reinvigoration of failing schools.

People and place

The interplay between people and place is at the heart of the city. It provides a central dynamic to what London is about, and it is mediated through the quality and the quantity of the built environment. London no longer has its nineteenth-century slums: some were bombed, some were demolished post war. The tiny brick cottages still seen across much of the erstwhile industrial North barely exist in London. To recreate the locations for the BBC series *Call the Midwife*, they used Chatham Dockyard: a historic location, preserved but not lived in. On the other hand, the locations for *Made in*

Dagenham, the film about the fight of women for equal pay in the Ford car plant, were at least partly in the same estates (the Mardyke in Havering) in which the women of the time were living. *Call the Midwife* is about the 1950s, while *Made in Dagenham* is about events a decade later. Even so, the factory has now disappeared and a Hoover factory in Wales, going through closure, was used as the factory location.

Low-quality housing in London is more likely to be in poor tower blocks and 1960s maisonettes, built to low standards and with inferior facilities, than in nineteenth-century housing. Even where this was badly built in the first place, the middle classes have come along and shored it up.

The post-war vision of garden cities required the (close to forcible) relocation of the poor to new places, to which the jobs would also be moved (also forcibly). Even in the 1970s it was necessary to have an Industrial Location Certificate to establish a new factory. But it did not work. The garden cities are not full of people walking to work. They are full of people walking to the station to commute to London, just as the villages of Surrey where I grew up had become dormitory towns for an earlier generation.

The new train lines we are currently building can create new opportunities to build liveable houses near the stations, but it is not at all clear that the planning system takes such opportunities into account. Neither, of course, does transport planning take development opportunities into account, but that is a matter for the next chapter.

Creating places in which people want to live is not the same as creating places in which people want to work. Nor do planners always grasp that what people want might subvert the plan. Patrick Abercrombie was the architect of the post-war London plan that saw the establishment of the Green Belt, the establishment of new towns outside it, and the vision for ring roads and radial routes. This vision has been undermined by the changing economic environment, the production technologies that made cars available to all, and the changes in family life that made it possible for women to go out to work.

The built environment – buildings and their arrangement – needs to be flexible. This is just as important as a flexible economic environment. As needs change, so too must the response. Abercrombie's vision was implemented in Plymouth, and he destroyed as much medieval building as the bombers did. Most people now regret this wiping away of the past and the wide car-friendly streets that were created. The example of Croydon, exactly the kind of suburb that must be made an attractive – as well as affordable – place to live, shows that it is not easy to implement a reinvention, navigating through the thickets of planning and incumbent interests.

Planning is important and necessary, but it needs to allow flexibility for London's different areas to change their character and their populations over time, and it urgently needs to address the problem of a shortage of housing of acceptable quality for those on a lower income in the capital. The housing market and the labour market are linked, and if the housing market problems are not fixed, London's economy will experience neither flexibility nor growth.

The planning process must recognize changing needs and uses, even if this sometimes means abandoning past assets and costs. These are sunk costs, which cannot be recouped. Nowhere is this more obvious than in the redevelopment of our major train stations, the subject of the next chapter.

Chapter 4

Infrastructure: King's Cross and St Pancras

One branch of the Northern line goes through King's Cross, the station where a fire killed thirty-one people in 1987, the second worst accident in the history of the Underground. The Northern line was also long known as the misery line – though new rolling stock has improved its reliability of late.

It is not only below ground that things have improved. There has been massive investment in and around the two adjacent stations of King's Cross and St Pancras (Figure 4.1): in the stations themselves, in the train services and in the surrounding area – an area that was once known for being a centre of both the drugs trade and prostitution. Development is underway to turn the area between the two stations into a new destination, with offices, shops and, no doubt, plenty of cafés, leading up to redeveloped warehouses at the north end, housing the Central St Martin's College of Art and Design.

The new concourse at King's Cross, a steel fan springing up in front of the original station, has won awards and is becoming an immediately recognizable image. Next door at St Pancras, it now seems inconceivable that the confection that is the station hotel was once listed for demolition and only saved by a campaign led by John Betjeman. The grand staircase is no longer derelict, only used for atmospheric music videos.

Figure 4.1. Vision of completed King's Cross and St Pancras development. Courtesy of Argent Developments.

This redevelopment does not come cheap. The renewal of the historic fabric of St Pancras and the insertion of the Eurostar station, along with the opening up of the station cellars that were once used to house the products of Midland breweries, have been extremely difficult and expensive processes. The shed roof of King's Cross station has new glass and ventilation systems that meet both modern standards and the requirements of English Heritage. Wonderful, certainly, but is it worth it?

Has the investment into these London stations created more than the sum of the parts? The answer depends on how important transport and other infrastructure are for the continuing success of London – this is not a straightforward question.

In this chapter I argue that our conventional methods for appraising long-term investment in infrastructure miss some of the hard-to-quantify benefits that the projects can bring. While London is investing in some key projects, such as Crossrail, it faces bottlenecks in other parts of its infrastructure, such as electricity and water supply.

There are two distinct but related issues that we need to explore. One is about how perceptions can shape decisions about where to visit or invest, as well as affecting quality of life. The other is about connectivity, markets and what makes a city productive.

If London is a world city, it would seem axiomatic that it needs world-class infrastructure, but this leaves unstated what this consists of. London's look and feel is one of its main assets. Compared with many modern cities, London is not very dense. Much of its built infrastructure predates the elevator, and it shows. This low density is also made possible by the public transport system: the Underground and the train network bring people into the employment centres from a considerable distance. The shift in economic geography already described moved around a million jobs from the edge of the city to the centre. This has only worked because the buildings could be built and the transport system had (just) enough capacity.

It is true that no one is yet employed to push people onto trains, as happens in Tokyo. But the system can still be enormously crowded. Standing on Platform 9 of Clapham Junction station at 8.30am on a weekday, you see as many people streaming off the train as are trying to get on – and it is standing room only both before and after. Those trains go to Waterloo, the busiest station on the network, seeing 100 million passengers every year.

This commuter network has grown in symbiosis with the city. I was born and brought up in Surrey, where every day my friends' parents got the train to work in the City. I was local: my parents were part of the society of small engineering workshops that supported the aerospace industry and the shopkeepers, solicitors and accountants of a market town. But we were also connected to that wider network of income-generating activities in what was then, fifty years ago, a more distant London. Now, the M25 has embraced my mother's house and we are part of the London conurbation, but still with a distinct identity. And the aerospace industry is long gone – but that story is part of the next chapter.

The remaking of the termini at King's Cross and St Pancras is not just about improving the stations to make them appealing consumer and passenger experiences; it is also linked to the improvement of the services. If the two do not go together, then the payback is limited.

We need to examine what form the payback might take. How can we establish whether an investment has been worthwhile? If the connectivity is not relevant, we might as well close the stations and redevelop the sites, which, after all, have a huge land take. In *The Fields Beneath*, Gillian Tindall traces the history of Kentish Town, from Domesday to the 1970s, nearly 900 years. It is startling how great the community disruption was from the railway land-take when the lines to Euston were put in. And while you can cross a road, crossing a railway is a very different proposition. Nonetheless, the disruption had huge benefits since these railways made it possible for cities to sell their products worldwide and started the acceleration of economic growth.

Identifying the payback to any kind of infrastructure is surprisingly difficult. The returns are diffuse and dispersed. These are known as general-purpose technologies – and separating out their impact from the impact of everything else is very hard.

Tim Leunig, an economic historian at the London School of Economics, has pointed out that when there is a distinct and identifiable shift – opening up new territories in the United States, for example – it is possible to pinpoint the change and the development thus catalysed. Even here, many other features are necessary to take advantage of such possibilities. People need to be willing to embrace the opportunity, and they need the skills to do so. Both capital and organizations will need to be mobilized. Indeed, Alfred Chandler, in his magisterial work on the development of the US economy, argues that it was the combination of the railroad and the telegraph that made modern corporations possible. The railroad could move the goods and the people, while the telegraph moved the management information and the manager's instructions. And, of course, they operated in symbiosis because the telegraph wire was carried beside the railroad track.

Leunig also points out that the other place where it is possible to identify the real impact of a piece of connectivity is where it releases a constraint. This is the case for Crossrail: a new railway currently being constructed under the centre of London that will link Heathrow with Liverpool Street, Essex, Canary Wharf and Kent. The argument is that there is untapped demand for people to work in central London – and to continue the shift from the periphery to the centre – but that the capacity of the system to deliver them is lacking. Indeed, a map of the crowded links shows that even with current levels of usage, crowding is a close-to-impossible issue. Crowding is not in fact very well defined: there are a given number of seats, but it is almost always possible to find a part of a train that is not fully loaded. People do not distribute themselves evenly along a train, getting on or off at different points, so a particular link might be very crowded until a number of people leave, only to get crowded again one stop further along the line.

The crowding heat map shows that even with modest growth, the system could reach a real pinch point, with the risk that it takes so long to get people on and off the train that gridlock is reached. We already see occasions when access to stations is restricted because of platform overcrowding; this could become commonplace without an increase in capacity. The result is the Crossrail project, conceived in an effort to relieve station crowding, to relieve pressure on the termini by allowing trains to cross London without requiring a change, and, particularly, to give resilience to access to Canary Wharf.

That last aim is actually a latecomer. Both Crossrail 1 and Crossrail 2 were identified as being needed in the 1980s, and the lines have been safeguarded since then, incidentally creating planning blight in the process. It has taken from then until now to start on the first line, and the second – crossing north–south and relieving stress at Clapham Junction, Waterloo and Euston, among other stations – is just emerging as a live proposal. Consultation on this new route closed in August 2013.

Since the pressure is obvious, we must ask why it has all taken so long. We must digress into the sorry saga of decision making, cost overruns, case making – and the Jubilee line.

The Jubilee line

The Jubilee line was originally built to relieve congestion on the Bakerloo line. This in turn resulted from the success of the Metropolitan line. It ended at Charing Cross and incorporated some services and track previously run by those lines.

Its more recent history has, however, been about creating development opportunities rather than relieving congestion. In this, it resembles the Metropolitan line, which created a successful feedback relationship between the development of the line and the land, where purchasers of houses knew they would be able to access work. While the recovery from the 1930s Depression is sometimes credited to housebuilding, even more important was the growth in jobs in new industries, which allowed people to purchase these houses. The line offered access to the new factories along the North Circular as well as to the centre of London.

Although the Jubilee line extension was not so much about new housing, it was certainly about new jobs. After much argument, the line south from Charing Cross was planned to go to Docklands – as we have seen, a major focus of regeneration – then on to North Greenwich and then back to Stratford: all locations where heavy industry had closed. However, the plan did not meet the required tests in transport terms. The Department for Transport has developed a battery of cost–benefit analysis tools to measure whether or not a project is worthwhile. These were then – and to a great extent still are – based on an analysis of the time savings to be made by those people projected to want to travel between A and B. In the case of the Jubilee line, the passenger numbers were projected to be relatively small and, hence, the time savings that would result, although substantial, did not cover the heavy costs.

In the event, a political decision was made to override this extensive modelling of trip-time savings. The then prime minister, Margaret Thatcher, agreed to the proposals of new developers in Docklands that their high-density proposition was a good idea, and that it would need a proper tube line for access, rather than relying on the existing Docklands Light

Railway, which had been planned for much lower-density activity. So there is a question about the validity of the detailed analysis and how it is used. A similar argument is ongoing today over the benefits of the construction of the high-speed rail lines between the north of England and London.

Construction of the Jubilee line extension, however, ran way over budget, with the final cost of £3 billion being twice the original estimate, worsening still further the apparent case for the scheme. The escalation was exacerbated by the subsequent decision, under John Major and ratified by the subsequent Labour government, to build the Millennium Dome at North Greenwich station, which necessitated a drop-dead finish date of 31 December 1999. Such firm deadlines always bring risk, and there are numerous anecdotes in this case of additional payments being made behind the scenes to ensure delivery. The consequence was considerable disquiet about the ability of the government to deliver large projects on time and/or on budget. HM Treasury now imposes 'optimism bias' on costs to reflect these risks at an assumed rate of 50 per cent – an estimate largely drawn from the experience of constructing the Jubilee line extension.

More recently, this disquiet has been somewhat allayed by first, the delivery of the high-speed line from the Channel Tunnel to St Pancras and second, the Olympics. While the eventual budgets of both of these projects were larger than the starting estimates, much of this was due to changes in scope rather than item costs. Not only have two large projects now been delivered on time and on budget but a third, Crossrail, is likely to follow suit. This has added to willingness to contemplate such major projects as the reconstruction of London Bridge station (Figure 4.2).

However, this was not the case with the Jubilee line extension, so, on the original analysis, the line should have been

Figure 4.2. A vision of the new concourse at
London Bridge. Courtesy of Network Rail.

a financial and economic disaster. In the event, this is not so.
Usage of the line is well in excess of the expected levels. A
seventh car has already been added, earlier than originally envisaged. When the finance director of Transport for London
was asked at a conference that I organized a few months before this car addition how long he thought it would take for
the new carriages to fill up, he responded 'about 45 minutes'.
Experience has shown he was right. The original modelling
suggested that the maximum use of the line would be 170 million passengers per year in some hazy future. It currently car-
ries more than 213 million.

All the evidence suggests that there is excess demand
for travel in the centre of London, and that new employment opportunities can be generated where there is good
access and the right built environment. One of the areas of
heaviest use of the Jubilee line post expansion is westward
from Waterloo into the West End and Westminster. Such use
was not predicted by the initial modelling. Indeed, a rerun

of the cost–benefit calculation, knowing both the costs and the passenger usage, shows a positive, rather than the original negative, result. Moreover, development has proceeded apace around new stations that offer that opportunity – notably London Bridge (Figure 4.3), Southwark and Bermondsey – as well as at the expected locations of Canary Wharf and Canada Water. London's tallest building, the Shard (Figure 4.4), now sits adjacent to London Bridge rail and Underground stations.

Figure 4.3. London Bridge Quarter development area (The Shard, The Place and London Bridge station). Courtesy of Sellar/Network Rail.

Even so, there is a subsidy. Usage may be well up and benefits may exceed costs, but these are 'economic' rather than financial benefits. The costs of running the Underground and the rail system are in excess of the fares collected. Indeed, a recent study has shown that London gets more public transport subsidy per head than elsewhere in the country. It is a pity that the study does not also point out that the usage of the system is higher, that the subsidy is spread over far more miles of travel, and that the taxes generated are also higher. It is a good example of a failure to take the broad view.

Figure 4.4. The Shard. Courtesy of Christopher Rosewell.

In broad terms, the fares cover the cost of operating the railways, but they do not cover the full cost of maintaining and improving them, let alone the cost of new investment. The case for these subsidies is not always clearly made, because of the confusion caused by the calculation of benefits in time savings.

Investment or saving

Focusing on time savings is relevant only if two strong assumptions can be made. One assumption is that the economy is independent of the transport system's availability and capacity. The other is that the calculated value of time savings is equivalent to the value translated into economic activity. If these assumptions do not hold, and it is hard to see why they would, then we need to think more carefully than we currently do about why as a society we should invest in transport schemes.

A current project where this argument has become live, and indeed heated, is the investment in Crossrail. This is now under construction and is due to open in 2018 (originally planned for 2017, but put back a year to save money – an example of the benefits of not having a drop-dead date). In this example, the standard analysis did show a positive ratio of benefits to costs, but the size of the project – a cash budget then of £16 billion – made paymasters very nervous, particularly over concerns about cost overruns and the recent Jubilee line extension experience in 2002, when the case was being presented.

Yet the instincts of the scheme's promoters were that this investment would be good for the economy and would have a real payback. One proposition would be to set the fares at a level to ensure this in financial terms. The difficulty with this is that no other part of the system was priced in this way, and half the network benefit would be lost if the new railway were not part of the overall system allowing easy interchange with other lines. A working group I chaired at the GLA looked at the whole question of how the line should be financed (that is, how the money should be borrowed) and funded, (essentially the question of how to pay back the loans raised to construct the line). If the loans can be paid back, it does not matter whether these loans are private or public, except that the cost is lower on government stock. We assumed, as a starting point, that there would be some subsidy on fares, and this was a social decision to prevent higher-value customers crowding out those with lower incomes and less ability to pay.

So the question becomes whether or not the transport system facilitates sufficient extra growth in incomes and employment to generate tax revenues to pay back the debt raised in a reasonable period of time. More generally, the question can be framed to include the operating costs too: are the levels of economic activity made possible by the transport system generating continuing tax revenues to pay for the subsidy to the system? The answer to such a question is highly contested, and there is no general consensus.

Economic theory provides little insight into this question because it deals poorly with questions of interdependence and feedback. Economic models generally describe equilibrium outcomes. They fail to identify the processes by which we might arrive there, or the time that it might take in practice. In these theoretical worlds it is hard to allow for the proposition that, for example, a transport system or the built environment can constrain the ability to deliver growth, and that there are feedbacks over long periods between transport, growth and buildings. Thus, in London, there are places with good connectivity which are nonetheless poor because the nature of the built environment makes it difficult to generate new activity. And some would argue that deprived communities should have such access even though there will not be comparable benefits.

The right level of subsidy is, thus, both a question of social justice and of economic benefit, intimately entwined. Fundamentally, a subsidy requires someone elsewhere to make the money to fund it. The transport system can manage this internally if the system itself creates the additional value.

It is easier to see this in the case of a new investment. This is the case that I developed for Crossrail. In essence, being able to deliver more people into central London enables them to do more productive jobs that would otherwise go begging. Indeed, these new workers would have a small effect on the productivity of those already there, because increasing the scale of this dense and effective agglomeration of high-quality people will raise everyone's game. The productivity effect is the result of a number of factors, first identified by one of the fathers of economics, Alfred Marshall, in the 1890s. He argued that a larger city would have more effective labour markets, would enable new activities to get going more easily, facilitate knowledge transfer and energize competition. Unfortunately, economics then forgot about all this, especially since many of these factors are about dynamics and change, which the subject still struggles to incorporate.

It has been left to geographers and the more imaginative to look for evidence to support these intuitively plausible propositions and to show that there is a relationship between city size and productivity. It is even more surprising that the Department for Transport, while accepting this argument, still struggles to accept that the transport system has a role to play in generating city size, preferring to believe that this relationship is captured in assumptions about time savings.

In the case of Crossrail, I showed that the additional taxes generated by the investment would cover the costs of building the railway. We focused on the constraints imposed by limitations of accessibility on activity across the central area of London and on the new centre in Canary Wharf. We used a number of modelling strategies to triangulate the potential effect. The London-wide transport model could be used to give one a sense of the transport choices people might make. It can be used to fix the future places in which people may live (based on borough plans) and to consider how places of work might shift, given shifts in available routes. This provided an estimate of 35,000 additional commuting trips into central London, and this in fact became the central estimate on which benefits were based.

Two other methods gave similar results, but were harder to turn into headline numbers as they developed over time. One (mine) looked at capacity constraints and developed a deterrence model based on some observations of when people delay getting on a train. On this basis, increased crowding increasingly deters trips, and this builds up over time. Another method generated a model based on a monetary value of time in a wage equation, in which net wages fell as crowding costs rose, and this would deter people from travelling. Although different in motivation, these models produced similar results in broad terms, with increasing crowding, absent the investment, preventing people from being willing to take up jobs in the centre of the city.

How much is this worth? If productivity is higher, then wages and profits are higher and tax revenues also higher. Argument was and is rife on how to value this. Accounting frameworks try to split out, for example, the returns to a person's skills and attributes from the returns to where they work. An unresolved debate has been about the difference between 'localization', which is about particular sectors, and 'urbanization', which is about density per se.

If I go to work in a village, are my skills exactly the same as those I exercise in the cut and thrust of the city? We know that people walk quicker in a city, perhaps they think quicker too. My own view is that the attempt to slice and dice the returns to particular elements in an accounting framework is misguided and misleading. While my personal attributes might be independent of the location in which I live and the industry in which I work, the development of my skills and experience and the value that I create is most assuredly not. I sit writing this in Monmouthshire, looking out into the woods of the Wye valley. But my ability to write it has been honed in the argument and contact of London, and indeed other cities. A post hoc accounting framework might be able to divide my contribution to output (if any!) between my education, experience and industry, but it could not be predictive in any useful sense.

Feedbacks mean that the static description may not tell us anything much about the future, which will require much more careful thought about how these interactions could take place.

There are two challenges, therefore, in thinking about the payback to infrastructure investment. One is to establish what constraints are imposed on future developments by not undertaking the investment, while the other is to value the consequent growth. Fortunately for London, the state of crowding makes the constraint pretty clear. The map showing how it would increase with even fairly modest growth provides a powerful illustration. While the valuation is contested, even fairly restrictive assumptions would give considerable benefits. And, moreover, the peak capacity of Crossrail is 70,000 trips over the three-hour morning peak. Only half of these were taken to be additional in the analysis that made the case for Crossrail, with the remainder being seen as transfers from other more crowded lines. If one believes, as I do, that it is likely that the rest of the system will in fact remain pretty much as crowded as it currently is, then this is an underestimate and there is scope for massive upside in the estimates.

The lesson of history is this: the cost–benefit analysis of the Victoria line suggested it would not be full until around the year 2000, having been constructed in the 1960s – a wildly incorrect prediction as it turned out. Thinking about investment in terms of a financial payback has an important lesson. It shows that this is not a zero-sum game. Debt can be paid off, and new debt capacity generated. Growth-enhancing investments do not reduce the capacity to invest elsewhere. Too often, no distinction is made between different kinds of investment, and debt capacity is not set against the assets being invested in. This is a common public sector mistake, since the assets for the public sector are essentially the taxpaying public, with no thought being given to the taxable capacity.

This section has focused on transport infrastructure, but there are other important infrastructure requirements. For example, electricity distribution is increasingly under stress with increasing data needs in many areas, including Soho's film-editing capability. In the water sector, London and the South East more widely is short of supply.

The Olympics

This all goes to show how the interdependence of cities' infrastructure investments will be a controlling factor in their success – which brings us to the Olympics. I am an Olympics cynic. Of course it was a great show. And there may well be external effects I admit to having underestimated. Two, in particular, are significant. First, we showed ourselves that we can deliver such an ambitious project not just on time but also on budget and in a controlled way. No last-minute panics; no poor standards of care or management. The transport delivery using public transport worked terrifically well. The renewed confidence this engendered is enormously important, as is the experience of this delivery for the teams involved.

Second, we should not underestimate the international impact of showing the world a successful Britain, one not just about theme parks and historic houses. As a shop window, this was an unparalleled opportunity. The mayor rose to the occasion by turning the café and meeting rooms of City Hall into a marketing suite and organizing investor meetings. Whether enough was made of this more generally is perhaps a moot point.

While these effects are both unquantified and, perhaps, unquantifiable, I am more dubious about the regeneration pay-offs that were trumpeted as the original justification. It is true that the Westfield shopping centre was built sooner than it would otherwise have done, and was able to take advantage of bridges across rail tracks and good access from stations and from Stratford. This had a positive pay-off.

I loved the park, and the planting (Figure 4.5), and I hope it will be well maintained. But as a regeneration benefit? The Olympic village has the potential to be good social housing, but we didn't need to stage the Olympics to build social housing. The argument about the future of the stadium and its unsuitability for football use tells its own tale about the extent to which the expenditure will yield only a short-term pay-off. Many have said that the Olympics made it possible to undertake investment that would not have been done otherwise, such as in the new rail access and stations. This does not seem to me to be a very good argument, and the Olympics as such was a distraction from longer-term needs. To say that only an event such as the Olympics can generate the necessary focus for these projects seems like making the best of a bad job.

Figure 4.5. Olympic Park planting. Courtesy of Christopher Rosewell.

Over the longer term my economist's cynicism might be misplaced. While I doubt that the claimed benefits will materialize, unclaimed longer-term ones might. This is about the fabric of the city, and the quality of the environment. Joseph Bazalgette is my hero here. As chief engineer of the Metropolitan Board of Works in the 1860s, he designed, and raised the finance for, London's sewerage system. This intercepted the open sewers discharging into the Thames and redirected the effluent further downstream (treatment plants came later). His great contribution was not just that he separated effluent from drinking water, but that he insisted on much larger sewers than anyone else thought necessary. He worked out the greatest need for the highest current densities and applied that to the whole city. Then he doubled it. The long-term pay-off has been huge, as it is only now that we are having to reinvest in the sewerage system, 150 years later.

Such long-term pay-offs do not lend themselves to our current methods of decision making. Our modelling for infrastructure needs relies on limited histories and short-term futures. The kind of risk analysis that Bazalgette undertook in building London's sewerage system ('What if we need more of it later?') does not fit into these approaches. It is remarkable how we pride ourselves on our investment analysis and yet the infrastructure seems to creak. Long-term decisions are made without much consideration of long-term risks and potential.

Nowhere is this more evident than in aviation policy, which is vital for London's international links as a trading city. It is time to look at Heathrow.

Chapter 5

Global city: Heathrow

Heathrow is unique among the airports of major world cities in that it is both smaller and closer to the city centre than any other. As a result, it is overused and creates more noise pollution than any other. One-third of all the people in Europe who suffer noise levels of more than 75 decibels live near Heathrow. It is the busiest two-runway airport in the world, operating at almost 100 per cent capacity. The prevailing winds mean that most aircraft descend to the runways right over the centre of the city, every ninety seconds (Figure 5.1). This is risky. Five years ago a flight from Beijing just scraped over the fence to an emergency landing. A few hundred yards sooner and it would have come down onto houses.

The selection of Heathrow to be London's international airport in the 1940s is shrouded in mystery and accusations of profiteering. The airport was little used in wartime, and the requisitioning of the site under wartime regulation has been described as a ruse to minimize compensation. The legal wrangles continued into the 1960s. Abercrombie (again) has been credited with the site's selection. But while other cities, such as Paris, have moved their airports as they have become busier and aircraft larger, Heathrow still sits there, crowding out alternative possibilities. In Paris, Charles de Gaulle airport was constructed in the late 1960s outside the city, and replaced Orly, much closer to the city, for international flights. Originally, the intention was to close Orly, though in the event it remained open for domestic traffic and currently sees 27 million passengers per year.

Figure 5.1. Low-flying aeroplanes. Courtesy of Christopher Rosewell.

Heathrow is ranked at number ten in the World Airport Awards, behind three European airports, Amsterdam, Munich and Zurich, and behind Singapore, Incheon, Hong Kong, Beijing, Vancouver and Tokyo. By passenger numbers, however, Heathrow is in the top three, with 70 million passengers in the year 2012, topped only by Atlanta and Beijing. Gatwick is number thirty-six, with 34 million passengers. Atlanta carried 95 million passengers in almost 1 million aircraft. Heathrow has less than half that number of aircraft, since numbers are capped. The effect has been to squeeze out smaller aircraft and connecting flights from smaller locations. If you want to go to a long-haul destination from, say, Newcastle, you will be more likely to travel via Schiphol or Frankfurt than via London.

Does it matter that Heathrow is so constrained and crowded? Or does it matter that it acts as a rather odd kind of hub, linking long-haul trips to each other rather than being able to collect short-haul passengers to make a variety of long-haul trips possible? As a result, it is possible to fly to a larger number of destinations from both Schiphol and Frankfurt than from Heathrow. What difference to London's future success would the expansion of Heathrow make? I shall start by examining the importance of air travel and its prospects. Part of this is the story of globalization, and the need to reach out to a wider variety of places, as well as encouraging them to reach in.

Trade is the lifeblood of any economy. Without trade and exchange we live at subsistence levels. Trade makes it possible to specialize, to exploit economies of scale and natural resources, and to reap the benefits of innovation. The more effective our trading relationships, the more effective our economies, and those of our trading partners. This is one of the basic propositions in economics, and one of the few that is not contested. Both theoretical descriptions and empirical evidence support the hypothesis that trade and growth go together. If we wish to grow, we must trade.

Of course, we might decide that we are rich enough, and that, therefore, more trade is damaging. Society might prefer autarky, and to live a more restrained life using fewer resources. Unfortunately, for the United Kingdom at least, this is not a real option. It is many generations since we were able to feed the population without imports. In World War II, even massive control of food production and intense rationing would not have prevented malnutrition, perhaps even starvation, without food supplies from the United States. The convoys across the Atlantic were Britain's lifeline. To return to any kind of self-sufficiency would be acutely painful. And the relative loss of welfare would be felt all the more deeply when other countries are continuing to grow and to develop new products and materials. Britain needs to keep up with these new materials and products; of the 7,500 patents registered for graphene, for example, only fifty-four are British, and the single biggest group is Chinese.

Moreover, the creation of added value is essential to the ability of a state to provide public services of any kind. If there is no income, there can be no taxes and no support for the services that a civilized society wants to provide for its citizens.

If trade matters, the next question is about what form it might take. In a large economy, such as the United States, it can be domestic. There is a great enough variety of people, geography, culture and climate to make this country a continent in itself. It is not surprising that the United States remains able to develop new markets easily and to innovate. Its margin of productivity over its nearest rivals remains as large as it was a century ago. Though the Chinese economy may be growing fast, its output per head is still only around 20 per cent of that in the United States.

For the United Kingdom, our global reach has been one of our major potential assets, even though we have let it slide for many decades. With a time zone equidistant between Beijing and San Francisco, plus the English language and a relatively well-educated workforce, we ought to be able to compete. London has been at the centre of whatever success there has been, but this should be a beginning not an end. Attracting investors from across the world should not just be about snapping up prime residential property, as is so often the reality, but about developing new worldwide business propositions.

There is no doubt that such investors feel comfortable in London, and indeed in the rest of the United Kingdom, but their willingness to arrive needs to be matched with more productive assets.

International connectivity is a key element in making this happen. Paris has flights to more Chinese cities than London does, although London is better connected with Hong Kong. Spain flies to more locations in South America than London does. These are the continents where growth is taking off, and the exports need to be made and the inward investors courted. Without direct connections, it is much harder to make trips and do deals, let alone follow on with delivery of goods. A third of Britain's exports (by value) are carried in the bellies of passenger flights. The goods follow the people.

Accepting that trade is central to economic well-being and that trade needs connections brings us back to the problem of how to provide for this. It is interesting that standard economics is of so little help here, as discussed in the previous chapter. Cost–benefit analysis would seem to provide a clear decision mechanism, but nobody agrees about the outcomes.

What is missing from the debate is a good understanding of the processes by which economies grow. Although the study of economics originally arose with the characterization of the division of labour in Adam Smith's pin factory, which was entirely about how productivity could increase and wealth grow, most modern economics has been focused far more on efficiency than on growth. This is puzzling. Surely efficiency and growth ought to be related: as pins are made better, they are made cheaper and resources are released to meet other needs. But growth also depends on being able to use more pins to make more and better dresses, create a new kind of sewing machine and develop new markets. The chasing of efficient outcomes in a static world, which is the preoccupation of cost–benefit analysis, will miss the larger story.

The triumph of the capitalist system is that it has allowed new things to be tried, experiments to be undertaken and failure to be managed, as well as success exploited. Such experimentation was central to the original cradles of the industrial revolution in Birmingham and Manchester. If you google 'Boulton and Watt' today, you will find a New York restaurant. But had Google been around in the eighteenth century it would have come up with a Birmingham firm of machine-tool makers. The firm was set up to exploit James Watt's designs for steam engines, and Matthew Boulton was the visionary who saw how the machines could be sold to manufacturers to improve their productivity. Indeed he also saw how new products could be designed that used the technology. Watt, on the other hand, had huge interest in engines but little in exploiting how they could be used. The combination of the engineer, the manufacturer and the salesman created a firm that lasted for 120 years. Capital was also essential. Expansion of the business was only made possible by the ability to borrow and the existence of banks from which to do that borrowing.

It is clear that this early industrial success was the result of a combination of factors coming together. In accounting terms it might be possible to allocate the success to capital, to skill and to scale. But, in practice, it seems doubtful that the removal of one factor would have left the same returns accruing to the others. It is the combination that creates the opportunity in the first place, and even then not all opportunities will be exploited.

Theories of economic growth have struggled to cope with this. They have tended to focus on decomposition of the measurement and have left the residual to what has been described, by some sources, as 'manna from heaven'. This is not good enough. The unexplained part is that which lifts the rate of growth from simply adding more people and machines in an existing technology to creating a twenty-first-century economy. Yet we know very little really about what combination of factors makes this happen, and economists should not assert that they know what the rate of growth will be in several decades' time – except to the extent that history suggests that most developed economies grow somewhere between 2 and 2.5 per cent per year on average. This does not explain how.

Even though we cannot well explain how this growth is achieved, we can say something about some of the main elements that are needed. We know that trade matters, and we know that innovation matters. So we need to allow scope for both trade and innovation to flourish, accepting that not everything will go well. Humans, and especially scientists, find it hard to accept that ignorance is widespread. Some years back, sitting on a committee responsible for awarding academic grants, the tension was obvious. Untried researchers would come up with innovative research proposals, which committee members worried would not work because they were untried. On the other hand, the focus of the research programme was innovation. Getting professors to accept it would be OK to give money to some projects that might not succeed was an uphill struggle.

Trade and innovation are unlikely to be spurred on by isolation and tradition. Watt might have invented his engine in a back room – though his ideas had, in turn, been spurred by the difficulties of the earlier Newcomen engine – but without Boulton this major improvement might well have languished in his workshop unexploited. And Boulton's utilization of it at the next step depended on the ability to exploit scale of production and the markets that could be entered both in the United Kingdom and elsewhere. Without these stationary steam engines, neither the railway nor the steamship would have been possible, nor the huge explosion of trade that these generated.

I have already described how cities can help generate innovation as part of the process of agglomeration. They also need to trade in the post-railway, post-steamship age, and this means air travel. Moreover, the new sources of trade growth are further away and more widely distributed than ever. The BRICs (Brazil, Russia, India, China) are being followed by other sources of acronyms, including Columbia, Indonesia, Vietnam, Egypt, Turkey and South Africa (CIVETS), and some countries, such as Malaysia, Thailand and the Philippines, that while not naturally fitting into an acronym are also growing fast. These countries are not all stable and can be high risk. But risk and reward should be part of taking hold of opportunities.

We need to reach these markets and they need to reach us without stopping halfway. This is what being a global city means. And this is what will maintain the returns that pay for environmental protection. It is true that poverty also protects the environment, but stepping back to such a point is likely to be even more destructive than trying to make enough money on productive things that we can afford to pay for the rest.

This is very relevant to the question of aviation connections because these are the trade-offs that the economic and growth debate ought to be addressing. It is not a technical debate about whether some future configuration of aeroplane production would mean that smaller airports might work. Nor is it about a preference for making travellers move between airports to make their connections. The future is not some nebulous mist: it is one step from the present. And in the present, our connectivity is not fit for purpose. World-class connectivity means large airports – whether in Beijing, Shanghai, Paris or New York. It does not mean shoehorning quarts into pint pots. Any expansion of an existing airport has consequences for those nearby. Any replacement of an existing airport with a new one will have consequences for new neighbours. These are long-term trade-offs that involve making judgements about the value of different environments and about the probabilities of different outcomes. Economists have little to say about these issues, but debate should still be able to inform them. Economists have produced lengthy evaluations of airports. Learning cost–benefit analysis as a student led me to the reports of the Roskill Commission, which spent much time and ink on where to locate a third London airport and started the cottage industry of stated preference and noise valuation. Stated preference is the activity of trying to establish what price people put on something that either does not exist or that has no market or price. For example, work has been done to establish how much Thames Water's customers are prepared to pay for a cleaner river if the Thames Tideway Tunnel is built. This works by asking hypothetical questions in various forms to get at these values.

Noise can be valued in this way, but it is clear that the valuations produced do not mean much to the participants. While the evaluation says that noise is much less valuable than travel, there are vociferous groups that do not agree. For them noise is massively important. It is not a question of the value of noise, but the value of a group. How is this to be weighed?

In the long term, what is value? Niall Ferguson has got into trouble for suggesting that Keynes's view that 'in the long run we are all dead' was the outcome of his failure to have children and his participation in a hedonistic and self-centred set – the Bloomsbury Group. We do not have to go so far to suggest that taking a short-term view is as much a cultural phenomenon as a real one. In the wake of World War I, in very uncertain times, many people became convinced by the dictum to drink and be merry, for tomorrow we die. Victorian investors, as we have seen with Bazalgette, took a much more optimistic and longer-term view, investing for their grandchildren as well as for their children.

Our current appraisal mechanisms are more in the short-term Keynesian than the visionary High-Victorian mould. For example, the methodology used to value our railway assets assumes that the useful life of the assets is thirty years. It is actually quite sensible to value the company that owns the assets in this way, since its value depends on its funding and the capital return that it must earn. But the replacement of all the assets would cost much, much more than the current valuation. Rebuilding London Bridge station will cost around £1 billion – and this does not include the costs outside the station, on resignalling and so on. But if it were necessary to acquire the land and then build the viaducts, bridges and cuttings that deliver the track, the price would rise astronomically. The same applies to Bazalgette's sewers. Their replacement cost is not counted. So infrastructure becomes the invisible asset. It is impossible to account for its value, or for the contribution it makes to the national economy.

Connectivity is just such an abstract concept. It requires physical infrastructure of all types. Although it is the ability to connect that we wish to measure, the infrastructure is not connectivity in itself. This remains invisible.

I have argued that trade and connectivity are intimately related to the economy and to our future in the world. Which brings us to the knotty problem of how to create and maintain such connectivity, whether with high-speed rail or with airports. Airports in particular are huge. An aerial picture of

London shows what a big bite Heathrow takes out of the city. Should it be there? Are there better long-term uses for this land, even if they involve short-term pain?

If in the long term our children and our children's children are alive, this is important. We may not be able to forecast the future, but we can and must make bets. My bet is that the process of globalization will generate increasing trade in services and increasing returns to innovation – industries in which the United Kingdom actually does well and could do better. We will never compete with Germany on machine tools. I, therefore, take the view that our long-term future requires us to be able to meet these growing market opportunities. This means increasing our ability to connect globally and, in particular, to have the range of options necessary to attract global players. We cannot risk being at the end of a branch line, vulnerable to future cuts in services. We are already perilously close to this.

An airport that attracts global players must live up to the standards set by the airports of other similar countries and locations. Such places are large, attractive and can handle the widest mix of aircraft. They can handle a variety of different incoming and outgoing patterns, with at least four independently operating runways. This is an important criterion – it needs an area of around 10 km by 5 km. The cheapest place to put this is obviously to the west of Heathrow, building across the M25 and a couple of reservoirs.

At least that is the cheapest option at first glance. But is it the cheapest option for our grandchildren, or just another fudge at decision making that takes the narrowest possible view? As one of the world's largest economies, we should be ashamed to be taking such short-term, narrow views of our future.

Ten years ago, I was asked to provide forecasts for London's employment for the following twenty years. Since then, there has been both a boom and a crash. I argued that a long-term projection should not try to forecast cycles, but should concentrate on trends and the reason for them. My team looked for productivity trends in major sectors of employment and used non-linear analysis to explore them. A relatively simple view of the future emerged. Fundamentally, this is a story of continuing growth in business-to-business services, buttressed by a continued willingness to invest in London from abroad and a judgement that people would continue to need to meet and talk and have offices.

So far those predictions have proved correct. I continue to bet that people need to get together, that globalization will not come to a juddering halt and that London's global attitudes will prevail. Once it is clear what the bets are, other judgements can of course be made. War, plague and pestilence can erupt. On the other hand, it would be mad, in my view, to fail to invest simply because of ever-present dangers. A failure to invest in the connectivity to keep our position in the world economy is a much bigger risk. This is why I believe we need to make sure that we have a world-class, world-scale airport. Large-scale airport investment is essential.

Where should such an airport be? On the whole, people do not like aeroplanes flying near their houses. On the other hand, though, people like to fly, and large numbers of staff are required to make an airport work. Trade-offs are clearly necessary, and getting the planes landing on runways off-shore makes most sense from the point of view of separating people and aircraft. But it only works if it is then easy to get the people there. So land-based terminals, with a variety of different routes to access them and a high-speed bullet train to reach the aeroplanes, may well be a good and effective compromise. Of course, giving people the option to stay away from the planes will be more expensive, but it also offers new development opportunities at Heathrow and to the east of London. To decide that short-term cost rules out such options would be crazy.

This is a UK view as much as a London-centric one. Some land-based airports will be useful, at Birmingham and Manchester, for example, as well as further north. But the land required for a major airport is huge and the island we live on rather small. Making use of the sea seems very sensible. And the most useful sea, for these purposes, is the Thames Estuary (Figure 5.2), so long as we can ensure good access by the right variety of means. For onward journeys, flying into the airport is a good option, with shorter trips being made by rail.

Figure 5.2. Estuary airport development illustration.

The most important aspect of this, however, is to make a decision and to implement it. Although my own position is that the estuary option maximizes flexibility and minimizes environmental loss, this is a debate without a 'right' answer. So in a sense it does not matter which option is selected as long as one is chosen and implemented at an adequate level of ambition. The technical debate is only part of the story. Different groups of people have different real interests and it is just as important to create a framework in which a decision can be made and accepted as it is to prepare highly technical reports. Without acceptance of the decision, implementation becomes problematic.

Currently, in 2013, this can be seen in the efforts to present the case for High Speed 2. The National Audit Office has rightly pointed out that the objectives of the scheme are not clearly articulated and that whether it meets these objectives cannot therefore be evaluated. The standard evaluation is based on time savings, so this procedure has been followed, with the result that opponents, unsurprisingly, criticize a scheme that apparently only reduces the travel time to Birmingham by twenty minutes. If the purpose of the investment were instead seen as the delivery of significant new connectivity to Manchester and Leeds, this would be a completely different context, but it would also require a different way of thinking about the benefits.

It is no wonder that politicians are losing their nerve when faced with an expensive scheme for which no one has yet put forward a comprehensive analysis and justification. I am helping with work on this proposal, and I do believe that additional connectivity between cities adds to the trade and growth case that I have outlined above. Only when there is no ambiguity over what policy is aimed at is it possible to make a clear decision and justify funding – whether public or private.

Unfortunately, discussions about the Heathrow question – like the other infrastructure investments covered in the last chapter – focus on the short term and the static, rather than on the long-term dynamics. Part of the analysis must be to ask what the alternative is. What will happen over the long term to the potential of London and of the United Kingdom as a global trading nation with key strengths in services if there is no significant new investment in international transport connectivity? We should not be willing to take the risk that other countries' investment in infrastructure and technology leaves us behind. It is not so much whether we can afford to stay ahead in global aviation as whether we can afford not to. Such an approach accepts that some things may prove to be underused. That is fine. Spare capacity is, however, an investment in competition, which spurs future innovation and growth. Continuously fully used capacity is a chimera of planners. Nothing stands still, we are all either growing or declining, forgetting or learning. Spare capacity is about space for the new.

In my youth I was a rebel, a Trotskyist. Trotsky coined the term 'permanent revolution' to get him over the hump that the revolution was not happening in the heartlands of capitalism, where it ought to, but rather in the world of the underdeveloped and agricultural. This made sense to me at the time, though I became disenchanted later. But the Trotskyist concept of permanent change definitely makes sense. Our investment and policy decisions need to acknowledge that change is unavoidable.

So in this world of risk taking, of permanent change and of the need for new investment, where should London stand? And where should the rest of the country stand with respect to London?

Chapter 6

Conclusions

In the period after World War II when London seemed to be failing, the cause was not other cities taking its role: other UK cities fared no better. And in the period of the great Victorian expansion, those other cities were just as successful. The great Victorian town halls with splendid brickwork, magnificent staircases and stained glass that stride across the North were being built just as London itself was being transformed. It is hard to pick a favourite amongst these amazing buildings – I particularly like Manchester's staircases, but Rochdale's fantasy brickwork is hard to beat. Apparently Rochdale's town hall was so highly thought of by Adolf Hitler that he instructed his bombers to avoid it, and while it may be an apocryphal story, it certainly appealed to the Lancastrian sense of humour.

London's relative failure during the post-war doldrums is a symbol of the loss of confidence in the country itself. The yearning for a more stable age, the power of the socialistic belief in planning, and the failure to get over the loss of empire all conspired to give us a generation of weak growth everywhere. All of Britain's cities tried to reduce density, bring in the car and build housing that it turned out people did not want to live in.

The more recent period, in which growth has recovered, has seen the recovery of cities everywhere too. Some have found it harder than others, but there is no evidence that a failing London would somehow secure the success of those that are struggling now. Allowing London to reach its potential, however, does generate income and activity that help both it and the rest of the United Kingdom. The big question, therefore, is how to make sure that London is best placed to make the most of the available opportunities.

Some might argue that all of this concern about the economy and the role of London is so much hot air – indeed, hot air that contributes to the danger of climate change. So far I have said little about this issue, and it can be a handy stick with which to beat anyone who talks about 'growth'. I want to make two points to get myself off this hook.

About twenty years ago, I vividly remember sitting on a panel charged with developing future scenarios, though I have entirely forgotten who had commissioned this talking shop. The memory is of the outrage expressed by the scientists who were even then making a career out of doom and gloom against the economists who thought that technology of various kinds stood a good chance of coming to our rescue. The scientists seemed unwilling to believe in human ingenuity, which had, after all, driven all of their own subjects. In the last twenty years, a rising focus on energy costs has given us a whole variety of new technologies, from wind turbines to solar panels, to tidal capture of various sorts. Shale gas fracking has also come of age. Technology may not completely solve our problems, but it certainly makes a huge difference.

The second point is about forecasting. I know a little about this, having been asked to gaze keenly into my crystal ball on many occasions. I have learnt humility. Our understanding of the laws of economics is pretty weak, our data pretty rubbish and the system complex, which means that small changes can have big consequences and big changes can have no consequence at all. Whether we are discussing economics or climate, we need to understand that we know very little. This is not an argument for nihilism. If there is a risk, it needs insurance. The risk of climate change should certainly be considered. It is not my purpose here to evaluate these policies, but to suggest that we should also consider the risk of undermining human responsiveness. People in cities can invent, develop and implement the new, which can respond to these challenges. Civilizations without cities do not exist. If London fails, it will be because civilization has failed.

The issues I have raised here about London's capacity to reinvent itself again successfully are all closely linked. While it is possible to increase density in the existing central area, the most effective investments in recent years have been around the edges. Following the first example of one of these developments, at Broadgate next to Liverpool Street, More London has redeveloped the southern riverbank between London Bridge and Tower Bridge; the King's Cross–St Pancras redevelopment has pushed out to the north; while Victoria and Paddington have helped to the west and south-west. The next candidate is Battersea, just over the river from Victoria, and spreading development west along the river from Vauxhall. It is of course notable that all of these fringe locations that have so far been incorporated into the dense and highly productive centre have good communications and can take advantage of train and Underground links. Indeed, in its reinvention, London got lucky. Just as there has been sufficient capacity in the Victorian sewer system to move effluent as the city grew, so there has been sufficient capacity in the Victorian transport system to move people around as jobs switched from the inner ring to the centre.

Although Battersea is very close to the city, it lacks that connectivity. The current proposal, to ensure not only that the city spreads out but also that the power station is preserved, is to extend the Northern Line into the site. Planning permission for the development has already been granted, but it now depends on planning permission for the Underground line. The government has already said it will guarantee the finance so now it rests with planning, and an inquiry, before there can be implementation. The long, drawn-out saga continues and is unlikely to be finalized before the middle of 2014.

Other city-fringe extensions are in progress. Shoreditch, as we saw earlier, is still up and coming, alongside such places as Earls Court and most major rail stations. Waterloo remains problematic. Its proximity to Parliament Square, which is protected by UNESCO World Heritage status, challenges the development potential, and planning permission is yet to be granted to replace the ugly 1960s development next to the station. Nor is there agreement about how to bring the disused international platforms back into use or how to manage access or track linkages. It is still all moving too slowly.

Extending the central area of the city is one priority and will require making the most of, and extending, its connections. However, there is also the need to improve connectivity across London. Some of these schemes were agreed to be necessary twenty-five years ago but now need to be considered in terms of their ability to support growth and opportunity, rather than just time savings. Connections outside London matter as much as those within it.

Crossrail 2 will connect south to north – we need to get on with this too. And London must urgently get a grip on our need for aviation as a factor in our international competitiveness, not just as a way to meet some assumed demand.

The heated debate about where London's airport expansion should occur must not turn into a sideshow; it is essential to reach a decision – on any one of the options – as soon as possible and get on with the investment and construction.

However, while infrastructure is necessary for growth, it is not sufficient. In the final analysis, it all depends on people.

Brains and brawn

I am trained as an economist, and it shows. My instinct is to think in statistics, in numbers and in terms of organizations. All the same, I know that cities are about people, businesses are about people, living is about people. People are about the relationships they have with each other and with the world. We are social animals. People respond to the incentives that they face and the situations that they find themselves in, and they do so in many and varied ways. The existence of politics shows that they do not agree about the appropriate ways to react to given circumstances, and particularly not about how others ought to react.

A lively and successful city is likely to be full of disagreements. In this sense it is the antithesis of the economist's equilibrium. Different people will be trying different new things and making and breaking arrangements to collaborate. Competition may be fierce, but it can also metamorphose into agreement. The attempt to find out what works will breed some successes and many failures, and each success will open up new opportunities. Such change can be disturbing. It does not seem fair that there are no guarantees that things will go well and that risk can be avoided. Unfortunately, life is not fair.

If the history of London teaches us anything, it is that change is endemic and the challenge is to keep up. Risk needs to be managed and mitigated but cannot be avoided. Those who, like William Cobbett, do not like change view London as a monster. Those who, like Samuel Johnson, delight in the cut and thrust of debate view it as a source of life and energy.

Maintaining energy levels is of course tiring. Some get burnt out, some need re-energizing from other sources. This is where diversity is relevant. London benefits from the diversity of peoples, cultures, skills and attitudes that it finds in its residents; this is an important way that reinvention comes about. The debate about immigration controls, therefore, draws a mixed response. On the one hand, people do not like disruption to their lives and locations. On the other hand, city residents understand change. A recent report by the Office for Budget Responsibility has suggested that immigrants make a positive contribution to public finances, largely because they arrive with their education already paid for. The report is much more agnostic on the contribution that immigrants make to productivity and output growth.

Some immigrant groups may make little contribution, failing to engage with the economy and society as a whole, while others may make a distinct contribution. And even within groups, individuals may also be very different. Skills, and the ability to deploy both brain and brawn, will be hugely important, as is the ability of the existing population to engage with newcomers – whether immigrants from abroad or those that come from elsewhere in the United Kingdom. When working with the Greater London Authority, I regularly asked how many in any audience were born in London, and it was never a majority. Asking who considered themselves a Londoner got a totally different response, regardless of accent, skin colour or country of birth.

In this book I have argued that there are four specific but linked policy requirements if London's next reinvention is to succeed.

- The effectiveness of the central business district as a location for changing activities and jobs needs to be ensured.
- Sufficient housing of decent quality has to be provided for London's workers.
- Investments needs to be made in improving the effectiveness of the commuter network and of other infrastructure.
- An early decision needs to be made to improve international linkages by airport expansion.

London can and does create Londoners that share a passion for their city and its business out of people born in a huge variety of places, from Bow to Beijing. This is the natural resource that will ensure that the city can remain a global city. All that remains is to create the stage on which this passion and energy can play.